A definitive guide to swimming through creative chaos, *The Storm of Creativity* shows us how to flow effortlessly through the process of birthing new, original ideas into the world.

—Joe Gebbia, Cofounder and Chief Product Officer, Airbnb

By picking up a book that forced me to think about creativity differently—*how DOES an architect think about creativity?*—I was able to enact the very things Leski suggests are necessary for creative thinking: abolishing preconceptions, thinking about form differently, making connections. Using *The Storm of Creativity* as a tool for meditation, for mind-opening, rather than as an instruction manual for creativity, I was able to pause and think differently about my own work.

—*The Chronicle of Higher Education*

This book is a refreshing and unique approach to understanding creativity. Leski refers to creativity in its broadest scope—architects, poets, dancers, scientists, engineers, chefs—anyone who brings to fruition an original creation that did not exist prior to their efforts. *The Storm of Creativity* is a wonderful addition to the literature on creativity and essential reading for all the various practitioners in the various genres of invention and discovery.

—*Leonardo Reviews*

Ever since architecture was conceived as a profession there has been a raging debateas to whether it is an art, based on a moment of quasi-divine inspiration, or a science, based on observations of the world. It is time that architecture is recognised for pioneering models of research that break down such unhelpful distinctions. This is the most important—if perhaps unintended—contribution of Leski's thought-provoking and very readable book.

—*Times Higher Education Magazine*

This is a book about the thoughtful journey of creativity. Life is about going from not knowing to knowing. This is the time of creativity. This theme, threaded throughout the book, is a source of confidence and terror all at once. It is how we give up comfort and preconception to discover the essence of design. You will enjoy reading Kyna Leski's illuminating account of the creative process.

—Richard Saul Wurman

I have always believed that a true creative process begins with a state of ambiguity because true creativity happens when it *deviates*, and your judgment can rely only on your level of impulse. In *The Storm of Creativity*, Kyna Leski vividly describes with precision and in a few words how such initial ambiguous emotion and imagination can become, from beginning to finish, a form of clarity.

—Wang Shu, Dean, School of Architecture,
China Academy of Art; 2012 Pritzker Prize winner

There is perhaps no intellectual who is as in tune with the vulnerability of the creative process and the uncertainty from which innovation emerges as Kyna Leski. Her focus on "unlearning" takes us back to our most elemental moments of learning as a child, but alsoto our most corrupted ideological predispositions. In her thinking, she develops critical mechanisms that braid the arts, sciences, and humanities to bring the various disciplines into conversation as part of the process of discovering. In this book, Leski brings the best of Cooper culture, as a school of thought, to a broader audience.

—Nader Tehrani (Dean, Irwin S. Chanin
School of Architecture, The Cooper Union)

THE STORM OF CREATIVITY

SIMPLICITY: DESIGN, TECHNOLOGY, BUSINESS, LIFE
John Maeda, Editor

The Laws of Simplicity, John Maeda, 2006

The Plenitude: Creativity, Innovation, and Making Stuff, Rich Gold, 2007

Simulation and Its Discontents, Sherry Turkle, 2009

Redesigning Leadership, John Maeda, 2011

I'll Have What She's Having, Alex Bentley, Mark Earls, and Michael J. O'Brien, 2011

The Storm of Creativity, Kyna Leski, 2015

The Acceleration of Cultural Change: From Ancestors to Algorithms, R. Alexander Bentley and Michael J. O'Brien, 2017

Mismatch, Kat Holmes, 2018

The Importance of Small Decisions: How Culture Evolves, Michael J. O'Brien, R. Alexander Bentley, and William A. Brock, 2019

THE STORM OF CREATIVITY

KYNA LESKI

FOREWORD BY JOHN MAEDA

The MIT Press
Cambridge, Massachusetts
London, England

First MIT Press paperback edition, 2020
© 2015 Massachusetts Institute of Technology

This book was set in Scala and Scala Sans by the MIT Press. Printed and bound in the United States of America.

Library of Congress Cataloging-in-Publication Data

Names: Leski, Kyna, author. | Maeda, John, writer of foreword.
Title: The storm of creativity / Kyna Leski ; foreword by John Maeda.
Description: Cambridge, MA : The MIT Press, 2016. | Series: Simplicity : design, technology, business, life | Includes bibliographical references and index.
Identifiers: LCCN 2015037746 | ISBN 9780262029940 (hardcover : alk. paper)— 9780262539494 (paperback)
Subjects: LCSH: Creative ability.
Classification: LCC BF408 .L47 2016 | DDC 153.3/5--dc23 LC record available at http://lccn.loc.gov/2015037746

10   9   8

to (s)p
—the b

CONTENTS

FOREWORD

John Maeda

I was presented with the opportunity to give a talk about design at an architecture firm in Boston shortly after I was appointed as president of the Rhode Island School of Design (RISD). Kyna Leski was someone I had heard about through an MIT colleague, so I looked her up and invited her to copresent with me. She accepted, and when she did so, I realized I had accepted a kind of risk as I had never met her before.

As a creative person, I am conscious of how I habitually (and still quite uncomfortably) try out new things as the only method by which I truly learn. For the talk, I stepped out of my comfort zone to invite a complete stranger into the occasion; at the same time, I noted how Kyna accepted my offer without hesitation. To me, it indicated that she was a person who was open to experimentation. I liked that quality, and recognized it for its kinship. And when I experienced Kyna presenting to the audience, I could feel something else in me: utter delight.

That feeling of delight from seven years ago has considerably multiplied on reading this work. It reads like she talks; Kyna speaks many dialects of knowledge—from engineering equations to achieve structural integrity to the perfect rhythm of a poem. Talking to her always reminded me of reading William Cuthbert Faulkner because there was always so much to gain from what she was saying as a barrage of free-flowing information, but I could easily miss how all the parts of what she was sharing were forming a whole. In fact, I once sent Kyna a little sketched portrait of her on a Post-it note depicted as a kind of tornado of ideas.

This book is an elegant deconstruction of the storm within Kyna's mind—as ten parts that form a whole. Each chapter provides a different perspective on the storm that lies at the center of her pedagogy for the creative mind, with no single perspective mattering more than any other. And although eminently readable as ten consecutive chapters, I can easily imagine randomly opening the book and starting from the page on which you land. It is *your* job to connect the dots provided across this book, for as Kyna points out in chapter 8, "Creativity is making connections or making the existing connections visible."

Since moving to Silicon Valley, I often hear the mantra "fail fast" as a key tagline of start-up culture. The underlying meaning of course is that it's important to iterate quickly when trying to launch a new creative idea. This is not different from what I've heard professed as an important aspect of learning, whether in my years at RISD or MIT. Even my book *The Laws of Simplicity*, which started this whole series for the MIT Press, has a chapter (and law) titled "Failure." So I find it particularly interesting that Kyna's book on creativity may be the only one out there that doesn't have a chapter titled or using the word *failure*. How can that be?

My guess is that like all good designers, Kyna has isolated the root at the root at the root, or as said in B-school parlance, she's answered "the five whys": "Why is it X?" "Because Y." "Why is it Y?" "Because Z."—repeated until there can be no more "because <blah>," and the core idea or issue has been found. Kyna started with and stayed with and ended with the storm, a literal force of nature. She's given us language to work with at the atomic scale, the atmospheric scale, the human scale, and with a healthy and needed dose of poetry and visual representations. Kyna has answered the question she first asks in chapter 2, "I might, as an architect, ask, How is the inside [of the storm] connected to the outside [of the storm]?" So be sure to leave your umbrella and galoshes at home, and go explore.

Kleiner Perkins Caufield & Byers

PREFACE TO THE PAPERBACK EDITION

Readers of *The Storm of Creativity* came from disparate backgrounds. I heard from musicians, businesspeople, students of design, software innovators, an oceanographer, a professor of science, Shakespearean scholar, painter, personal coach, and so on. Several wrote to me about the play of chaos in creativity as in storms and in the contribution of the creative process to outcomes that were unintended.

These correspondences inspired me to research the origins of chaos theory and its confirmations of the volatile nature of beginnings. Questions about intentions, where they come from and how they are formed, and our control over outcomes became the focus of my work since.

Unintended outcomes are not necessarily "bad." The truth is that most significant and beneficial discoveries are unintended. They are uncanny surprises outside of the expected: that is what makes them discoveries and inventions. They cannot be explained a priori. Their reasoning comes from their coming into being.

The story of my father's design of the chandeliers for the Metropolitan Opera is one example. He was working on a perspective sketch of the interior of the Metropolitan Opera House for a meeting between his boss, the architect Wallace K. Harrison; John D. Rockefeller; and the general manager of the Metropolitan Opera, Rudolf Bing, when an accident happened. His sketches were expressive; his drawing skills afforded him the courage and freedom to improvise, experimenting with mixed media and working quickly. In making the finishing touches of his sketch with paint, he carried a brush charged with paint over the page and a big splat of white paint splashed across the page. In an attempt to camouflage the splat, he connected lines from the splatter to make it look like the refracted light from a chandelier. The sketch was presented as scheduled and the group mistook the corrected splat as a design for a chandelier. That is how the iconic chandeliers of the Metropolitan Opera House came to be.

So where do intentions come from; how do intentions, which seem to emerge from the process, relate to the stated intentions at the outset; and how do we know which to follow or fuel? I wrote about this process in chapter 4, "Gathering and Tracking." One gathers to fill the space that was previously filled by preconceptions embedded in the initial intention. "The sensation is a clearly possessed sense of purpose often accompanied with the thought, 'I don't know what I am doing but I know I have to do this.'" This newly found sense of purpose begins the tracking of an intention that emerges from process. The last five years have allowed me a chance to dig deeper into these questions as well as test ways of gathering and tracking in arenas broader than design.

I have returned to the power of three active, in-the-moment, decision-making faculties:

- Improvisation (chapter 5): on-the-spot choices made through propelling recognition and generation of pattern and language
- Sensibility (chapter 6): live sensory feedback of perceiving and conceiving
- Imagination (chapter 7): the glimpse of an alternative to the here and now affording movement to move ahead.

These faculties are generally associated with the arts. Improvisation is a term and practice known to actors, comics, and musicians. And it is at play over a longer period, without a live audience, with the choices made by all artists and designers. But improvisation is necessary in any situation without a plan, script, or map, and when you find yourself in the unfamiliar. Improvisation is needed in crisis when on-the-spot and in-the-moment decisions are made and actions taken.

Creative people such as artists, clothing designers, and chefs are celebrated for their sensibility. But sensibility informs the surgeon as to how much pressure to apply to the scalpel. Similarly, the community organizer "reads" the room in regulating and directing pressure of purpose.

Imagination is associated with children, illustrators, and storytellers. But as leaders of the civil rights movement knew, it also fuels the courage to escape oppression by offering a counterweight to an existing reality.

Even though these faculties are vital, necessary, and practiced in addressing the most pressing problems, they are ignored by academic institutions. An increasingly data-driven culture occludes the immeasurable. Sensibility, improvisation, and imagination aren't valued in the writing of prescriptive syllabi—the guidelines of curriculum committees and myopic strategic plans—yet they are indispensable for uncertainty and crisis.

In the timing of this paperback edition, I have been asking the question, How does one form intentions that have consequences that extend in scope and scale? And I find myself circling back to the immeasurable faculties of creativity: sensibility, improvisation, and imagination. All three come from a personal and immersive relationship with the world that *The Storm of Creativity* invites.

ACKNOWLEDGMENTS

I am grateful to the MIT Press for publishing this book, especially executive editor Bob Prior, manuscript editor Deborah Cantor-Adams, and designer Erin Hasley.

Thank you to John Maeda for his laser vision and life support. I am deeply moved and grateful for your words that accompany mine.

I greatly appreciate the work Scott Cooper did alongside me, chopping up my writing and putting it together coherently.

Thank you to Jessie Shefrin, former provost of RISD. Jessie has integrity that is rare and endangered. And great appreciation to Laura Briggs, head of the architecture department at RISD, for her timely offer of support before I asked.

I am grateful to the friends with whom I have had conversations over the years that feed the storm. Thank you to Stuart Blazer, a poet, whose words can be found in chapter 7; the world would be a better place if more people knew his fine work. Thank you to

Friedrich St. Florian for his mentorship and friendship. Thank you to Kristin Jones, visual artist, for her inspiring and generous spirit; Thank you to David Gersten, thinker, teacher, architect; and to Richard Saul Wurman, the greatest connector I know. And thank you to Joan Richards, professor of history at Brown University and historian of mathematics, who acted as a spiritual guide in the past year.

I am grateful for the contributions from Frank R. Wilson and Elliot Washor.

Peter Lynch, architect, compared the storm to "proto reasoning" as we wrote the problem for the RISD core curriculum that came to be known as the "Block Problem." That problem and others written for the Making of Design Principles class traveled to other architecture schools worldwide. I am grateful to all the faculty members teaching this class for the contributions they made to its pedagogy.

To my students, I offer appreciation for their sense of purpose, especially those students who have since become my friends and colleagues; Jack Ryan, Olga Mesa, Marcus Shaffer, and Jonsara Ruth, to name a few.

I would like to acknowledge several of my teachers: Rosemarie Pantaleo Sheetz introduced me to rigor and precision in art; Thomas Depelteau taught me to think abstractly through geometry; John Hejduk spoke to my daimon; Robert Slutsky, the intellectual painter; Sue Gussow, who brought embodiment back to architecture after a cold, dry spell; Robin Evans, the architectural historian for architects; Rafael Moneo, architect; and Stephen Jay Gould, who changed my outlook on life.

I would like to acknowledge my father, Tadeusz Marian Leski, gifted architect, who taught me to draw from life as an essential process like breathing, and my mother, Iris Leski, who introduced me to poetry and acting.

Finally I have a debt of gratitude to Chris Bardt—architect, professor, colleague, partner, husband—for the quiet hydrologic cycle underlying it all.

This book describes the creative process—actually many processes that comprise a larger process—I have experienced and observed. I have listened to and observed these many processes as a teacher, student, maker, writer, and architect myself. I do not suggest these processes can be followed as a recipe for being creative. I simply want to describe what I have observed, try to convince you of its universality, and encourage you to recognize these processes in your own practice.

The many processes are really stages of an overall process one navigates in knowing, making, or discovering something that does not yet exist. These stages are not really something one can schedule or impose externally; rather, they are stages one experiences internally. And even though a stage may quietly commence internally for the creator of a work, it can be empowering or debilitating. Simply put, the creative process is bigger than you. It is like a storm that slowly begins to gather and take form until it overtakes you—if you are willing to let it.

That doesn't mean you don't have a critical role to play. On the contrary, like a little eddy that can trigger a hurricane, each individual causes a disruption that kicks into motion a purpose that gathers and sheds material and thoughts each day through expressions and choices made.

I am often asked the simple, innocent question "How do you *know?*" after avenues were pursued, doubts raised, preconceptions shed, frustration experienced, and a point of exhaustion reached. How does one know what to do, where to go, when it's right? In here you will find my response to that question, based on what I have observed about creativity.

This book is about creativity writ large. It is not an art or architecture book, even if I do use several architectural examples in the chapters that follow. My work and interactions with other architects, designers, painters, poets, educators, engineers, inventors, mathematicians, and scientists have given me some intense experience with how the creative process is navigated, and led me to an understanding of the creative process's essential stages. My observation is that these stages are essentially the same irrespective of whether the creativity is artistic, scientific, technical, business, or whatever. So my thoughts in this book could be part of anyone's conversation with the creative process. As the well-known author and speaker on education and creativity Sir Kenneth Robinson has written, "Creativity is not exclusive to particular activities; it's possible wherever human intelligence is actively engaged. It is not a specific type of activity but a quality of intelligence."[1] I am confident my observations of the creative process are universal.

One of the best views into the creative process is anything that documents the day in, day out work. Here you can see firsthand the struggles, doubts, hard work, revisions, revelations, leaps, and setbacks. Charles Darwin's letters have served many as a resource for seeing firsthand how he made the leap to connect principles in nature that were out in the open for anyone to see and connect, but how *his* work and frame of mind led *him* to make the connections that irrevocably changed not only biology but also our outlook on life.

Especially revealing are manuscripts that unself-consciously hold the reiterative cycles of creativity from a few notes to a draft and then multiple revisions. The book *The Making of the Pré* documents the four-year process that engaged French poet and essayist Francis Ponge (1899–1988) to write a particular poem.[2] It is a small portion of the manuscript of writings and rewritings made in the development of the poem or, as Ponge liked to call it, dense essay "The Pré" found at the end of the book. Although only a fraction of the actual manuscript, the book is *about* the creative process, and the hundred pages of *The Making of the Pré* are one of the best records of that creative process.

Pré is the prefix of prefixes, and present in "present" and "preparation." "The Pré" is about the creative process and beginnings. I owe a great debt to Ponge and that work for confirming and demonstrating through the recorded manuscript the workings I have observed in the creative process.

I have often thought that the onset of the creative process is like coming upon a clearing. *Pré* is also a reference to a meadow; the word means "meadow" in French, that generative soft ground, "less solid than nonliquid," solid enough, just enough to "appose one's foot." Like a meadow, it is a ground that is stirring and unsettled, a place of tremendous generative power, an opening that induces attentiveness or vigilance ... a pause ... a place of choices and setting out. That is a great description of the creative process as well.

What I didn't realize until I reread *The Making of the Pré* as I wrote this introduction is that in the four years of its making, a storm appears, breaks, and passes. Two years into the writing of the manuscript, Ponge describes the Pré as a "green incarnation of the rain," and describes the meadow's grass as pumps, with the "drop of dew on each needleful of green thread, ... the eye of the grass." Ponge says, "And from the initial raging storm, a gentle outcome, persistence and perseverance in gentleness."

I am, like many others, astonished by the role the unconscious plays in the creative process—how ideas seem to spring from nowhere. I had completely forgotten Ponge's metaphor of a storm. As you will see, forgetting, deliberate inattention to an agenda, or unknowing is a stage of the creative process. Equally important and the opposite of forgetting is the effort to try and see ahead.

We see ahead when we make designs that are materialized in the future, when we write problems that anticipate solutions, when we link one step to another in navigating our lives and the way through anything, especially the empty page, writer's block, confusion, chaos, needs, and questions. The creative process is the story of this passage and speaks for the author, to the user, the reader, inhabitant, audience, or viewer.

I think a few words are necessary to explain how this book and its chapters are organized. We think of process as something linear, but the creative process I describe here is not linear. Still, because a book is linear by virtue of having chapters that follow one after another, I have no choice but to describe the creative process along a linear path. I encourage you to think of it as *not* being linear but instead cyclic. Sometimes the stages of the cycle double back on themselves, and you find you are undoing what you have already done. (And in fact, even the stages within the process are themselves cyclic!) Some of the stages I describe can happen in an instant or take decades. Some cycles continue to produce and transform into a next cycle, and others peter out.

Creativity is a path with no beginning or end. What you create is never an end point. Creativity per se has no formal output; rather, it is an ongoing process.

Storm's-eye view.

CREATIVITY AS STORM

Create comes from the Latin *creāre*. It means to make, produce, or cause to grow. In other words, when something is created, it comes into existence. This means it is something new. The Latin word is related to *crēscere*, which means to arise; it's where we get our word for the crescent moon.

The term create is the root of the creative process and creativity.

Creativity has been at work for more than a million years, and the process itself and catalytic points in the creative process are essentially the same as always. What has changed, as civilization has grown more sophisticated, is *how* we are creative, especially the tools we use.

STORM

I invite you to look at the process of how something new arises through the metaphor of a storm, because I see the creative process as a storm.

How is the creative process like a storm? It begins from what appears to be nothing; this corresponds to moisture condensing and rising to form a storm cloud. For instance, the lift of the low pressure that begins the process of a storm leading to a hurricane seems to rise from nothing. The warm tropical ocean causes water molecules to collide, and some of these colliding molecules escape a liquid state and become vapor. The vapor condenses as it rises, releasing heat energy, and forming the water droplets and ice crystals of a cloud.

Storms arise out of a disturbance, and act to displace and destabilize. They gather energy and material. They gather force and direction. They propel and are propelled. They have consequences, from saturated ground to rainbows and all manner of other effects. And they have no discernible beginning or end. That is exactly what happens in the creative process.

The creative process is also like a storm in how it gathers direction, force, and intention from its particular situation. It is dynamic: it starts, stops, rages in one moment and abates the next, ebbs and flows. These are all characteristics of a storm.

Further, storms have different scales. They may be relatively large; they may be relatively small—from dust devils to sandstorms, rain showers to hurricanes. Regardless of their size, we can look at them at several scales. We can observe the creative process in the same ways.

Storms are contagious as well. So too is the creative process. Just as one storm feeds another, one person's creative practice can feed the creativity of another person. Storm and creativity both have fluid, unclear boundaries; you cannot draw a tight circle around a single storm, nor can you do so around a single creative process. When the hurricane is making its way across the Atlantic, its boundaries are constantly changing. None of the Weather Channel's computer models can capture the storm precisely.

A storm, like the creative process, is continuously in motion. Both are shaped by their conditions, just as their conditions shape them. They take in from their situations, producing and depleting again and again. The wind and water runoff from a storm shapes the landscape and topography; the temperature and moisture and landscape and topography shape the storm. A creative project grows out of the conditions, content, and forces of its situation. And a creative work meant to serve one purpose may transform into serving an entirely different purpose, each shaping the other. One creative work grows out of another, and they are reciprocal.

Reiteration is common to a storm and creativity. One iteration among the many of a storm's journey runs through a cycle along a storm's vertical axis. In the creative process as in a storm, the cycle includes editing and production. Momentum grows and wanes, fueled or depleted at moments along the path. In the creative process, this corresponds to the energy of the storm, which is produced and dissipates over and over.

There is a continual gathering of new material along the path of a storm; the cyclonic motion of the eye is the gathering system for the storm. Moisture and heat is gathered, fueling the storm. The same is true for the creative process. The momentum is greater than any single iteration. And just as the water in the ground left by a storm is part of the hydrologic cycle, beginning a new storm or, more accurately, keeping the storm going, the creative process starts itself all over again.

The consequences of a storm and creativity are real, and specific. They are found in the *exchange* that happens between the world, creator, and those with whom the creation interacts. This may be the viewer of a work of art, recipient of an idea, patient receiving the novel treatment, dweller in the built house, user of an artifact, and so on. Creation is, in this respect, truly "in the (mind's) eyes of the beholder," and the principal consequence of the creative process is transformation. As the great American poet Walt Whitman (1819–1892) wrote in *Leaves of Grass*:

All architecture is what you do to it when you look upon it;
(Did you think it was in the white or gray stone? or the lines of
    the arches and cornices?)

All music is what awakens from you when you are reminded by the
    instruments,
It is not the violins and the cornets, it is not the oboe nor the
    beating drums, nor the score of the baritone singer singing
    his sweet romanza, nor that of men's chorus, nor that
    of the women's chorus,
It is nearer and farther than they.[1]

Whitman is explaining that the consequence is the exchange with the viewer or observer or listener, not the building or music itself. Consider this tangible example of how much the creativity of science has changed our outlook on things. The phrase "sunrise and sunset" was in usage before Nicolaus Copernicus showed us that we on earth are doing the moving, not the sun. Our understanding of the universe has transformed since the Copernican Revolution.

I mentioned the rainbow earlier. It may be the most interesting and specific consequence of a storm, and is analogous to the specific consequence of the creative process: a phenomenon experienced by others. The creation of a rainbow transpires as rain refracts and reflects sunlight as it falls. A ray of light bends on its passage through the convex spherical surface of a water droplet, splitting into red, orange, yellow, green, blue, indigo, and violet light. The spectral rays pass through the drop and then reflect off the concave back of the drop and through and out on a different angle from where the light originally came. This is because the substance of water slows down the light, and the curvature of the drop bends the light as it hits. In other words, there is a collision of light ray to the curved surface of the drop that bends the light. The colored components of the light bend at different angles and speeds, fracturing the ray into the spectrum of colors and then reflecting off the back of the drop along different angles, sending each of the colored rays on its own trajectory.

All that specificity in the creation of the rainbow feeds the output, just as it does the creative process. One of those spectral rays meets the eye of the observer, but only if the observer is there to meet that ray. And only the rays that meet the observer's eye form the image of a rainbow; only the partial rays from the many drops that are coincident on the lens of our eye forms the image of a rainbow.

The arc we see in the sky is the cone of light that refracts back in line to the observer's eye. The rainbow you see is different than the rainbow visible to all other observers, because an entirely different set of drops refracts and reflects the light in alignment for each observer's eyes. The falling drops are only in position to perform this function for that very moment when they pass through that single ray of light. They continue to fall away, and other drops pass in place to refract and reflect light again. Falling rain suspends the rainbow in the sky for the short time that the relationship of sun, rain, and observer are aligned for the transformation to happen, and thus for this creative phenomenon to exist.

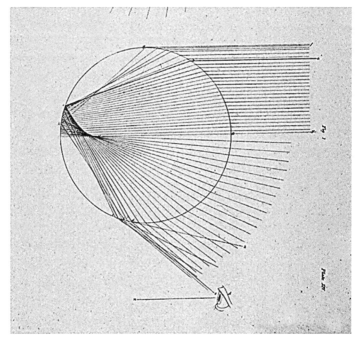

Graphic optics of light refracting through a raindrop.

NOUMENA AND PHENOMENA IN CREATIVITY

The English word *noumenon* should be more familiar. It is related to the word *phenomenon*; they share the suffix *menon*. *Pheno* means "of the senses" and *nou* comes from *noos*, meaning "mind"; together, the Greek word *phainomenon* means "thing that appears into view."

A noumenon, in its dictionary definition, is "the object, itself inaccessible to experience, to which a phenomenon is referred for the basis or cause of its sense content." In other words, noumena are formed in the mind as the aspects that conspire to bring about a phenomenon. Noumena and phenomena are at work in creativity, both in the process and experience of something created.

Phenomena are experienced events, such as rainbows and eclipses. The fact that someone is there to experience a rainbow or eclipse is what makes it exist. In other words, every day, someplace on earth, rain is falling with sunlight passing through the droplets. The spectacle of a rainbow depends on someone standing in line with the refracted rays of light to see the display of the spectrum. The beholder of the rainbow completes the phenomenon. Without the observer's retina and brain to collect the image, there is no phenomenon. It exists by being sensed.

The same is true of an eclipse, which absent an observer is an otherwise-insignificant event. After all, the moon and sun are always in alignment; it is the fact that at a given moment the alignment is collinear to some point on earth from which we can see it that makes it significant.

There is much more to the analogy between the two phenomena—creativity and storm. Creativity, like a storm, cannot be controlled. This is an important point that is central to the message of this book. Creativity can only be harnessed, to a degree. Just as a meteorologist cannot tell you how to make a storm, I cannot tell you how to create. I have, though, observed various stages and elements of creativity, and more often than not they are part of every creative process. I think that an understanding of creativity is served by understanding these elements. I believe you must acknowledge that, and accept these elements and their implications. It is something you can navigate, but you do not have complete control over the course. In a sense, it navigates you.

Like a storm, creativity is bigger than you. It begins before you know it. It is beyond your complete control. In each cycle of the creative process, it involves emptying your mind. That is the subject of the next chapter.

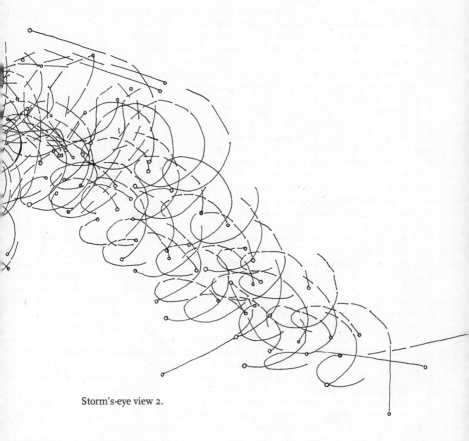

Storm's-eye view 2.

UNLEARNING

Creativity requires an open mind. An open mind springs from unlearning, which rids us of preconceptions. As the Greek Stoic philosopher Epictetus (ca. 55–135) observed, "It is impossible for a man to begin to learn that which he thinks he knows."[1]

Unlearning is like the storm's disturbing and agitating characteristics. It disturbs our sense of what we know. We are agitated when we discover we don't know, and that compels us to go forward in search of knowing. This is true irrespective of our field of knowing. Artists work freely with uncertainty and play, and accept the thoughtless and immediate "knowing" of intuition without the support of facts. Data are used not only to substantiate an intuition but also to spark further speculation and unknowing. As artists, we are surprised to find that scientists also work without knowing, sometimes following a hunch or aesthetic sense. The story that follows is an example of one that surprised me. It is about a scientist I once met on a flight to China who had a problem to solve and who explored without knowing why.

The microbiologist told me about making soil for planted green walls that stand about a hundred meters tall. He had found in the course of the work that plants don't like growing under glass. For a while, he wondered why, but he had since given up on finding an explanation.

I asked him whether it was because the air is trapped under the glass.

"No," he answered. "We tried putting holes in the glass for circulation."

I asked whether it was because of reflections or the optic properties of glass.

"No," he said again. "We just don't know why."

Finally, I asked whether it had something to do with the greenhouse effect.

"We just don't know," was his response.

And then he said something quite profound. "I have accepted that we don't know, and I can move ahead without knowing." I understood immediately. He was trusting in himself, following his own nose (so to speak), without giving into the need for a rational explanation for why he was doing what he was doing. It is part of being creative, but it is not always something scientists and engineers feel comfortable allowing themselves to do.

I once saw a bumper sticker on a car that read, "Don't believe everything you think." I celebrate that message as a necessary approach to the creative process. Unlearning is about questioning what you thought you knew. Say you are given a kind of creative assignment, like a client coming to an architect and asking for the design of a new dining room of a certain size and in a certain location in her house. That assignment has its solution already identified, based on a preconceived notion. With an open mind, though, you may discover that it is not the creative solution. Instead of asking her what kind of dining room she wants, you explore how she lives, how she prepares and has meals, what times she eats in the kitchen or prefers another space, what types of adjacent functions would work best, what kind of connection with the outdoors she would want, when and how she entertains, and so on, with no preconceptions that the solution is a dining room or even more general preconceptions about "room"?

Questions have a remarkable power to undo preconceived choices, disrupt assumptions, and turn your attention away from the familiar. All these lead to a more open mind. Instead of choosing where the window should be, I might, as an architect, ask, How is the inside connected to the outside?

If your starting point is to name and identify potential solutions before unlearning, it is unlikely to lead to anything creative or outside what you already know. At that point, everything you think of is based on preconceptions. That means they already exist, and creativity is about that which does not exist. That is the point of the discussion of phenomena in chapter 1 and the analogy to the storm. A creative process comes from displacing, disturbing, and destabilizing what you (think you) know.

ABOLISHING THE PRECONCEPTIONS OF BRAINSTORMING

This is a central principle: preconceptions hinder creativity. Creativity involves preventing yourself from making what you already "know." Creativity involves thwarting your own preconceived plans, abilities, and assumptions. Unlearning allows for a fresh perspective, like a forensic scientist throwing out everything he thinks he knows and saying, "Let's take a fresh look at this."

Therein lies another problem with brainstorming. It may well be that what someone shouts out in a brainstorming session may be a "fresh look" to you, but isn't brainstorming an accumulation of the preconceptions of every single person participating? Unless the entire group successfully went through some kind of unlearning to clear all the individual minds in that room, brainstorming has the potential to fill your mind with the preconceptions of others. When Alex Faickney Osborn adopted the military usage of the word storm to coin his term *brainstorming*, it didn't appear that the fortified place being assaulted was analogous to preconceptions.

American physicist Murray Gell-Mann (b. 1929), winner of the 1969 Nobel Prize in Physics for his work on the theory of elementary particles, made remarkable contributions to human scientific understanding. In his book *The Quark and the Jaguar*, he explains just how central this notion of getting rid of preconceptions is to the creative process, no matter the discipline.

> A successful new theoretical idea typically alters and extends the existing body of theory to allow for observational facts that could not previously be understood or incorporated. It also makes possible new predictions that can some day be tested. Almost always, the novel idea includes a negative insight, the recognition that some previously accepted principle is wrong and must be discarded. (Often an earlier correct idea was accompanied, for historical reasons, by unnecessary intellectual baggage that is now essential to jettison.) In any event, it is only by breaking away from the excessively restrictive received idea that progress can be made.[2]

I am convinced that you can learn to unlearn, to have an open mind. In fact, you must. And how do you begin to unlearn and get on the path to achieving a truly open mind? Let me give you an example from my own teaching at RISD.

Every year, we get a new crop of architecture students. They come from varied backgrounds, as undergraduates and graduates with undergraduate majors of every imaginable stripe. Some have studied art (broadly defined), and some have not. Some have backgrounds in the sciences, mathematics, literature, music, philosophy, business, medicine, the armed forces, and so on. They bring with them a whole host of preconceived notions. And then they enter their required first-semester design studio.

There, the unlearning process begins. We conceive the studio as a fresh starting point for everyone. All the students are given a daunting problem to solve, a challenge to surmount. The problem is chosen quite deliberately to take away whatever ground for reasoning, for making decisions, the students may have brought with them to school.

While each year's challenge is different, they all have in common that they induce questioning and making, simultaneously. There is no preparation. No methodology lecture precedes the assignment. No theory is given a priori. The students are in it to unlearn.

The students are given a straightforward but difficult problem. In the course of working on the problem, as you will see, they are compelled to unburden themselves, to free their minds, to lose their preconceptions. Whatever they thought they were certain of, or had wanted to do, soon falls away, giving way to uncertainty. Now to avoid despair, we do begin the problem with a bit of inspiration:

the students view cellular material through a microscope—an awe-inspiring sight.

Inspiration induces an open mind through the realization that there is something unknown that is palpable or on the cusp of knowing. I think the sensation comes from the realization that something unknown is close enough to intuit. Inspiration conveys a sensation of a clearing, an opening—an expanding sense of the open mind. That open mind creates space by virtue of the absence of preconceptions.

In creative practice, it is important to dwell in that space, because when you do so, absent your preconceptions, you learn to dwell in the uncertain. Whether you are an architect, artist, scientist, engineer, or whatever your discipline, that uncertainty is necessary for creativity. It is like the instability necessary for the onset of a storm.

UNCERTAINTY

In a letter to his brothers George and Thomas written in 1817, the English Romantic poet John Keats (1795–1821) wrote of the importance of uncertainty in creative practice.

> Several things dovetailed in my mind, & at once it struck me, what quality went to form a Man of Achievement especially in Literature & which Shakespeare possessed so enormously—I mean Negative Capability, that is when man is capable of being in uncertainties, mysteries, doubts, without any irritable reaching after fact & reason.[3]

Having an open mind is usually associated with a readiness to entertain new ideas. But what I mean by an open mind goes well beyond that notion. I mean a readiness to have no ideas, a true tabula rasa, a genuine blank slate. When I take on a new architecture project, I ask questions that induce uncertainty about whatever "answers" were the givens of the project. My objective is to sit with the empty table or blank page. I want to have an open mind, and uncertainty gets me there. Uncertainty is key to growing and moving beyond what you think you know. If you are certain, you cannot have an open mind, and therefore you cannot create something new. And if it is not new, it is not creativity.

Doubt, insecurity, questioning—these elements of uncertainty become critically important. The unburdening creates an opening.

The students who viewed the cellular material under the microscope were given the assignment of building a three-dimensional structure from what they saw, using a stubborn or temperamental material. I chose the material because I knew it would not respond to anything imposed on it; instead, the students had to listen and respond to the material. They had to pay attention to what it could or could not do, and work from there. A stubborn material is indifferent to what I might want or the students might want. It prevented them from making what they knew in a way they knew, because the stubborn material wouldn't allow them to do what they planned on doing.

In my mind, the lesson here is not unlike the "exploitation of errors" Jerzy Grotowski taught at his Theater Laboratory founded in Poland in 1959. Grotowski rethought the nature of theater. His teachings and art has influenced directors, actors, and anyone interested in performance ever since. He thought of the body as the material an actor has with which to create. Mistakes are, in essence, expressions of the unpredictable and temperamental nature of his "material."

Grotowski taught his actors to work with mistakes as opportunities for discovery. Any involuntarily movements, word pronunciations, or lines were to be incorporated rapidly into the creative structure of the actor's role. The intention wasn't to teach the actors to hide mistakes but rather for them to learn improvisation by working with the unintended actions and vocalizations. Improvisation is performance of the present tense. Unscripted, it is a responsive art of what develops in the moment, as opposed to following a script. It is a live form of creation.

Likewise, a stubborn or temperamental material wants no part of any preconceived plans, and acts out. You need to work (with) it. It occupies a place between those necessarily discarded preconceived plans and the idea revealed by the material to the students who must build the three-dimensional structures.

By taking on the assignment, students unlearn their preconceptions, achieve an open mind, and follow the detours the process takes. This is why I like the artist's word for the material with which they work: medium. A medium is something that goes between. A medium is also something that transmits. It goes between the preconceived and revealed idea.

Students given this assignment may feel as if they've been thrown into the deep end of a pool or shipwrecked, but everyone survives. Still, as the Spanish philosopher José Ortega y Gasset (1883–1955) wrote in one of his many essays,

> To be shipwrecked is not to drown. The poor human being, feeling himself sinking into the abyss, moves his arms to keep afloat.[4]

The peril those students feel as their preconceptions disappear is a good thing that helps them achieve an open mind. Ortega y Gasset continued,

> Some discontinuity must therefore intervene, in order that man may renew his feeling of peril, the substance of his life. All his life-saving equipment must fail, he must find nothing to cling to. Then his arms will once again move redeemingly.

Still, with all those feelings of peril, the students move forward. They begin to make, and the clearing of their mind forces them to pose important questions about their making. Since the challenge they've been given has no cues to trigger prior learned methods or preconceptions, some ask, "Is this what you want?" What I want is not the purpose of their education. They don't get an answer. They have to move their arms and swim on their own. Returning to Ortega y Gasset:

> This movement of the arms which is his reaction against his own destruction is culture—a swimming stroke.... When culture is no more than this, it fulfills its function, and the human being rises above his own abyss. But ten centuries of cultural continuity brings with it—among many advantages—the great disadvantage that man believes himself safe, loses the feeling of shipwreck, and his culture proceeds to burden itself with parasitic and lymphatic matter.

Ortega y Gasset was writing about the making of a culture, but his message is universal to creative practice, which contributes to the making of culture. Culture develops authentically as a process in its making. If culture is understood as a preexisting complete condition that sits as a context for design, then design is not a result of the creative process but instead is based on connoisseurship. In other words, the objective would be to meet the standards of cultural conventions or tastes.

With preconceived notions, you simply confirm. With a truly open mind, you make discoveries because you are open and aware. My students come up with amazing ideas about structure and space and order that they later incorporate into their architecture. I like to think it happens because they are enjoying a particular kind of "state of grace" I myself experience when I achieve a truly open mind. In that state, I do not know what I am doing, I do not know where I am going, but I do know that I have to take the journey and follow wherever it goes. The thoughts that come from this state are small notions, accepted tentatively, but accepted because that is all there is to hold on to. I have referred to these early notions as "rafts" that one builds out of the flotsam of the sea of the unknown. Flotsam that comes to mind, for no apparent reason, but that is all you have after being thrown from the shipwreck of your preconceptions.

Still another approach to unlearning is to tackle a problem in a way that undoes one of your skills that you may otherwise use as a crutch (since a crutch is just another form of a preconception). For my students, this could be having them draw with their nondominant hands, so that by losing the swiftness of dexterity, they have to be very much in the moment, observing carefully what is happening as they draw. The great Swiss painter Paul Klee famously advocated turning one's drawings upside down midway in their making, then continuing to draw, and then returning to the original orientation and reconciling the differences. As Klee wrote in his "Creative Credo" (and the same could be said of the creative process generally), "Art does not reproduce the visible; rather, it makes visible."[5]

Close-up of joinery of collapsing wire structure.

The idea of clearing your head and opening your mind reminds me of Charles Darwin's (1809–1882) discoveries when he took his famous voyage on the HMS *Beagle*. Darwin was not the "official" naturalist on board; rather, that task fell to Dr. Robert McCormick. Captain Robert Fitzroy had sought another naturalist as a companion for the journey—someone who the captain saw as a kind of social guest on board with whom he could enjoy conversation. Darwin, of course, took the opportunity to engage in the work of a naturalist quite seriously, but the "unofficial" aspect of his presence created a more relaxed and open-minded environment in which he could observe, without official obligations to fulfill. The three

Wire structure that can collapse.

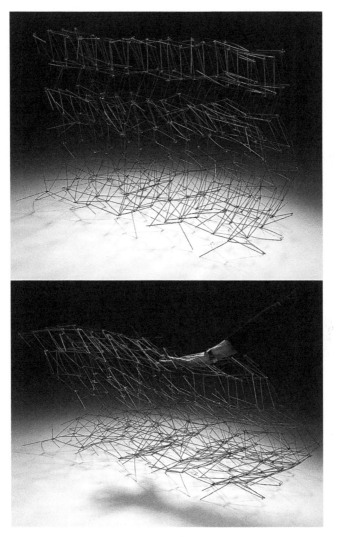

Wire structure that folds like an accordion.

Wire structure with expandable and contractable properties like a sponge.

principles of natural selection Darwin developed on the voyage are a great example of discoveries right out in the open that could only be seen with an open mind cleared of preconceptions so the relationships could be seen. The result: a major paradigm shift in the human understanding of our world (as well as an excellent example of "connecting," the subject of chapter 8, where I take up Darwin again).

ATTENTIVENESS

It is the uncertainty that comes from unlearning that induces the attentiveness of which the legendary Nadia Boulanger (1887–1979) wrote. She was a French composer and conductor, but is best remembered as the teacher of many of the twentieth century's leading composers, including Elliott Carter, Aaron Copland, Virgil Thomson, and many others. I remember she thought attentiveness was a necessary attribute of musicians but one that could not be taught. I disagree. I think the entire process of unlearning puts you in front of what is happening in the moment, and hence makes you more aware and attentive.

Attentiveness is a key element of creativity. With a clear, open mind, you cannot be trapped in a focus on what you already know or think you know. That tendency to embrace preexisting ideas gives way to a focus on the here and now. The open mind induces attentiveness to the process, to what is happening at the moment, to the work at hand.

Attentiveness in the creative process deemphasizes information that already exists and what you and others may have done before.

It also de-emphasizes the pressure to reach after the fact and reason Keats mentions in his letter. It leads to new ideas.

As they appear to you, new ideas are unfamiliar. Unfamiliarity induces wonder or fear. Ask yourself, "What could this be?" Don't worry that fact and reason may not help you fully understand the unfamiliar. I am advocating that you dwell in the uncertainty of the unfamiliar and unknown. Let it create receptivity to new ideas that your preconceptions may once have blocked.

N. Joseph Woodland (1921–2012) offers an outstanding example of attentiveness in the creative process. While you may never have heard of Woodland, his invention "adorns almost every product of contemporary life, including groceries, wayward luggage and, if you are a traditionalist, the newspaper you are holding," wrote the *New York Times* on the occasion of his death.[6]

Woodland was neither an artist nor architect. He was an engineer. As a graduate student in mechanical engineering, he was enlisted by a fellow student, Bernard Silver, to take on a problem that had been presented by a supermarket executive who visited Drexel University in 1948 looking for someone to develop an efficient way to encode product data. Woodland and Silver worked on a number of ideas, none of which were workable. But Woodland was convinced he could come up with the answer. So he quit graduate school to devote himself to the task, moving to his grandparents' home in Miami Beach. That winter, he sat on the beach in a chair, thinking about what to do next.

Part of his process was clearly to empty his mind of preconceptions. That does not mean emptying your mind of everything you've ever encountered or learned but instead abandoning the effort to reach after fact and reason that leads us to "stock-in-trade" answers to questions that may not have even yet been posed.

Woodland realized that he would need some kind of code to represent information visually. He had learned Morse code as a Boy Scout. The *New York Times* story continues: "What would happen, Mr. Woodland wondered one day, if Morse code, with its elegant simplicity and limitless combinatorial potential, were adapted graphically? He began trailing his fingers idly through the sand."

The *New York Times* obituary quoted from a 1999 article in the *Smithsonian* magazine in which Woodland told his story.

> What I'm going to tell you sounds like a fairy tale. I poked my four fingers into the sand and for whatever reason—I didn't know—I pulled my hand toward me and drew four lines. I said: "Golly! Now I have four lines, and they could be wide lines and narrow lines instead of dots and dashes." Only seconds later, I took my four fingers—they were still in the sand—and I swept them around into a full circle.

The circular pattern was preferred because Woodland reasoned the code could be scanned without having to be oriented in a certain way.

In 1952, Woodland and Silver were awarded a patent for what they called "Classifying Apparatus and Method." It took time before the invention could be used widely, because the original scanner was too large and expensive. Eventually, one of Woodland's colleagues at his eventual employer, IBM, designed the black-and-white rectangle version of the bar code, "based on the Woodland-Silver model and drawing on Mr. Woodland's considerable input."

ISBN 978-0-9960747-0-4

I am convinced that Woodland's momentary abandon while sitting on a beach chair, his attentiveness to the here and now that resulted from having cleared his head, is what led him to draw his fingers through the sand and make his discovery, which solved the problem and enabled the invention of the Universal Product Code, or UPC. "In retail establishments worldwide they are scanned at the rate of more than five billion a day," the *New York Times* obituary noted. "They keep track of books in libraries, patients in hospitals and nearly anything else, animate or inanimate, that will serve as an affixable surface. All because a bright young man, his mind ablaze with dots and dashes, one day raked his fingers through the sand."

Woodland teaches a great lesson for creative practice. His story shows the critical importance of dwelling in the uncertain rather than the insistent, willfully reaching after fact and reason. Perhaps that is why he left the environment of Drexel University to pursue a solution to the bar code challenge. Like my students with the challenge I described earlier, Woodland came to accept his own uncertainties and then developed a temporary raft to sail atop them. A raft has little room for baggage.

In the final paragraph of *The Great Gatsby*, American novelist F. Scott Fitzgerald (1896–1940) conjures the confrontation of the unexplored from the perspective of the thoroughly explored and settled landscape of Long Island. Gatsby is standing on the North Shore at sunset, looking out along its coast:

> Most of the big shore places were closed now and there were hardly any lights except the shadowy, moving glow of a ferryboat across the Sound. And as the moon rose higher the inessential houses began to melt away until gradually I became aware of the old island here that flowered once for Dutch sailors' eyes—a fresh, green breast of the new world. Its vanished trees, the trees that had made way for Gatsby's house, had once pandered in whispers to the last and greatest of all human dreams; for a transitory enchanted moment man must have held his breath in the presence of this continent, compelled into an aesthetic contemplation he neither understood nor desired, face to face for the last time in history with something commensurate to his capacity for wonder.[7]

Even when the task at hand is to build on existing achievements, it is important to create in your own mind the proverbial blank slate through questioning. It matters in every creative endeavor, whatever your discipline, even if in reality you cannot avoid your mind being inhabited by some of what came before your work, and as one engineer has written, should not:

> We engineers are often accused of being uncreative. In fact, many nonengineers would say that the phrase Creative Engineer is an oxymoron. Why is that, since much of engineering is inherently creative? If we weren't inventive, how could we ever develop new technologies and adapt emerging scientific principles to solve problems? ...
>
> First, let's start by defining *creativity*: it's the quality of making, inventing, or producing—rather than imitating—and it's

characterized by originality and imagination. One reason engineers aren't considered creative is that they often don't start with the proverbial blank sheet of paper each time they do something. Rather, they build on existing technology and try to improve incrementally on its performance.[8]

You'll need to make space within your mind to look deliberately beyond what (you think) you know. Space needs to be made for wandering—and wonder. Clear your mind, and be ready for ideas and a journey in the direction they point. As poet T. S. Eliot (1888–1965) wrote,

We shall not cease from exploration
And the end of all our exploring
Will be to arrive where we started
And know the place for the first time.[9]

In an interview, Gell-Mann told of a time when he made a "mistake" and identified it as a source of discovery. He was asked about a time he had a revelation that led to him being able to explain strangeness, a central part of particle physics. Strangeness is a property of particles—expressed as a quantum number—that describes their decay in strong and electromagnetic reactions.

I had come up with an incorrect explanation, which had some features in common with the correct one, but which was wrong. And I knew why it was wrong. And another fellow had gotten the same idea, and figured out that it was wrong, and had ... published the idea, plus the reason why it was wrong. But in a very confused manner, so that it was extremely hard to follow. I hadn't even read it, but I knew what it was, because I had the idea, and I knew why it was wrong. And when I visited the Princeton Institute for Advanced Study ... the theoretical physicist there asked me to explain how this worked, how the idea went and why it was wrong. And I said yes I can do that. So I went to the blackboard and I started explaining the idea, and explaining why it was wrong. Part way through I made a slip of the tongue and I realized that the slip of the tongue made it ok, the arguments against no longer were valid, and this was probably the right answer. That was how I found the strangeness theory.[10]

As I see it, what made it possible to Gell-Mann to solve the problem was the very thing that enabled Woodland to do so. He was relaxed, not trying to solve his problem, which created a kind of awareness that had not existed before. He wanted to say "five halves," but it came out as "one" instead. Reminded by the interviewer that those two are "not even close, in language," Gell-Mann replied,

It's not close in any way. But one worked and five halves didn't. So obviously there was some interesting mental process going on out of awareness. The problem was being solved, and the solution was being stated, by a mental process out of awareness. And it came out on a slip of the tongue. Shrinks would love that, I guess.

Antoni Gaudí (1852–1926), the Spanish Catalan architect, is an example of someone who used a creative approach that came from unlearning. His masterwork is the Sagrada Família, a large Roman Catholic church in Barcelona. The construction of this church, designed in the Gothic style, had begun in 1882 under the direction of a previous architect for three years; Gaudí was commissioned to take over the project.

Imagine the expectation Gaudí must have felt to be dutiful to the Gothic style of the cathedral now in his care to finish. He delved into a deep inquiry about Gothic architecture, which led him into a creative process that took the structural inventions of Gothic architecture a few steps further. He did this by forgetting Gothic architecture as a style. Rather than employing stylistic elements according to a literal architectural historic approach, he asked probing questions about Gothic architecture's structural principles. Why was the style the way it was?

Sagrada Família.

Forgetting as part of creativity is something embraced by other creative people. French philosopher Gaston Bachelard (1884–1962) quotes the French poet Jean Lescure (1912–2005): "Knowing must therefore be accompanied by an equal capacity to forget knowing.

Non-knowing is not a form of ignorance but a difficult transcendence of knowledge. This is the price that must be paid for an oeuvre to be, at all times, a sort of pure beginning, which makes its creation an exercise in freedom."[11]

The world of business offers a compelling argument for unlearning. In a *Forbes* magazine article, one business leader advocates it be taught in business schools. Her definition of unlearning isn't exactly the same as mine, but it's worthwhile to consider, especially since so many business schools teach students using case studies, unleashing those same students into the business world as managers and consultants who then try to replicate the case studies in their work. Erica Dhawan, a consultant and author on leadership and innovation, writes, "Unlearning is not exactly letting go of our knowledge or perceptions, but rather stepping outside our perceptions to stand apart from our world views and open up new lenses to interpret and learn about the world."[12]

As Dhawan further advances, "We need to embrace ambiguity and uncertainty more in business school." That is, indeed, part of the path to creativity.

Lescure advocated forgetting in order to know—a form of unlearning. Gaudí's own unlearning led him to structural inventions of his own, to his own style, to something that had never existed before. In chapter 5, "Propelling," I explore how Gaudí did this by employing material and structure. First, though, let's look at other components of creativity: problem making, gathering, and tracking.

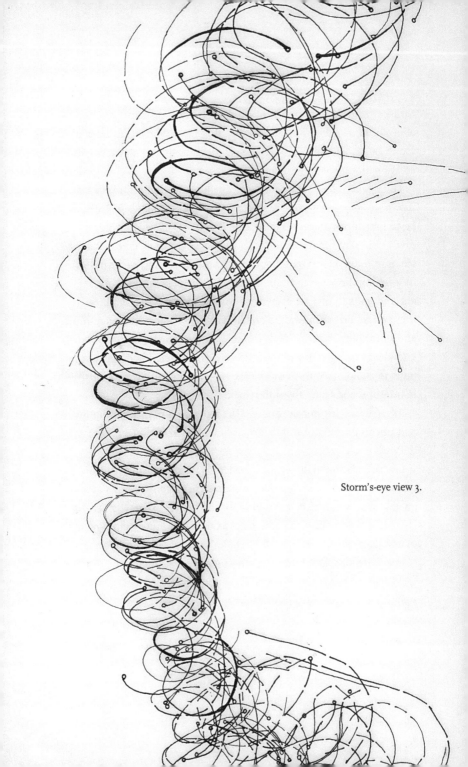

Storm's-eye view 3.

PROBLEM MAKING

When you rid yourself of your preconceptions through unlearning, you leave an absence. That absence creates both a need and awareness. The need is the want to know, induced by not knowing something or no longer "knowing" what you think you knew before. That leads you to attentiveness to what is before you, an awareness of the here and now, like Woodland experienced on that Miami beach.

Unlearning unfolds in a way that creates. When you realize you don't know something, you have created a problem—specifically, the problem of having a need to fill. Because the problem didn't exist before, you can rightly say you made the problem. That need, that void from unlearning, creates an impulse to know—an impulse that like the problem, didn't previously exist. The impulse is to know something that is much more specific than what you thought you were working on. It sets in motion the direction, intention, and content for the process. It is the dynamic of the process.

The American poet and teacher Richard Hugo (1923–1982), describing a creative act, wrote, "It contains and feeds off its own impulse. It is difficult and speculative to relate that impulse to any one thing other than itself."[1] I don't think you can inherit a creative impulse from another or anything that precedes it. The impulse Hugo describes is inextricably linked to the creative act. While it is problematic to speculate how that impulse was caused by any one thing other than itself, one creative practice may be linked to another and a broader context of practices by each individual's own need to know. One line of thinking may be exhausted and abandoned by one author, artist, or scientist only to be revived by another's own impulse. This may seem obvious, but to the individual who is ignited by an impulse there is a real sense of an autonomous, anonymous invitation to begin. There is a sense of a small privilege to have received that impulse, and that if not seized, you will miss something, a small opportunity, an unturned rock. There is a sense that because you received this impulse, it is your responsibility to act.

Some problems may be made by working on one thing, and suddenly discovering something else that creates a need to know, a curiosity, and a need to satisfy that curiosity. Some of the greatest creativity has resulted simply from doing something, setting out to discover, with an open mind. Take continental drift. Alfred Wegener (1880–1930), a German geophysicist and meteorologist, noticed that the same rocks comprised the coasts of continents opposite each another, separated by an ocean. He surmised that this was evidence that continents once whole had drifted apart. On his expeditions, Wegener collected rocks as evidence.

Wegener's theory was earth shattering, literally. It was controversial in part because there was no known mechanism to explain how it could be possible, how continents perceived as so solid and massive could drift across the ocean. It simply seemed absurd.

A half century later, the British had a machine that in addition to its original purpose, could dig up rocks from the ocean floor. So they just started digging. They dug up a lot of rocks and found something curious. When igneous rock cools from a molten state to a solid one, it locks in the direction of magnetic poles at the time of hardening. Geologically young rocks are found close to the oceanic ridge, where the oceanic plates meet and spew magma. Older rocks are found farther away, because the spewing of the molten rock pushes these older, already-hardened rocks away from the ridge. The British scientists found a shift of magnetism depending on whether the rocks were dug up close to or farther away from the oceanic ridge. What they found was evidence that the magnetic poles had flipped in the millions of years between the formation of the young rocks near the ridge and the old rocks farther away. It was something they could map. This was the development of paleomagnetism; the scientists had found a substantial basis for Wegener's hypothesis.

At about the same time, the Japanese were pursuing similar things. They had lots of problems with earthquakes and were trying to figure out why. The British shared some information with the Japanese, and a theory of plate tectonics emerged. Basically, the shifting of the magnetic poles found in the rocks on the ocean floor was the evidence for the violent shifts of plates that explained what made the continents drift. The theory of plate tectonics used today was created with all sorts of important implications for the human understanding of the earth.

Wegener's problem of needing to explain why the continents drifted didn't exist until he made his observations in the field. A work of creativity creates its own necessity. Once it exists, we need it. Once Wegener had established a theory based on something he observed, found curious, and had substantial evidence to support, the problem could transfer from one creative practice to another.

Problem making is like the stirring of the storm. Stirring creates an unstable weather condition that initiates the storm, just as problem making initiates creativity. In one sense, the creative process can be expressed as a simple equation:

the creative process = wanting to know something you don't know

In other words, through the creative process you make something to know something.

As a meteorologist, Wegener was a great observer. He was used to observing natural phenomena. When he noticed the similarities in rocks on opposite continents, it created an impulse to know what could make the continents drift. Wegener made that problem a part of his creative process. But he never lived to see his problem solved; others solved it for him. He collected the evidence of corresponding rock formations from one continent to another, but died unsatisfied on a glacier during a polar expedition.

By digging up the ocean floor, the British were unknowingly solving the problem Wegener created. And the Japanese brought it all together with the theory of plate tectonics. This is a good example of how creativity is not isolated, that the impulse of one problem leads to a process, which feeds a need to know, which leads to another problem. Like weather systems, one storm is never isolated from the processes that lead from the previous storm and to the next one.

This is not to say that all creative work must be integrated into a lineage of tested ideas. As Bachelard wrote, "The poetic act has no past, at least no recent past, in which its preparation and appearance could be followed."[2] Wegener's discovery also had no past, but its significance had to be realized: others had to connect their own work to that of Wegener.

DEFINING A PROBLEM

In his book *The Quark and the Jaguar*, Gell-Mann wrote this about creativity, raising what is involved in defining a specific problem:

> Sometimes a correct idea, when first proposed and accepted, is given too narrow an interpretation. In a sense, its possible implications are not taken seriously enough. Then either the original proponent of that idea or some other theorist has to return to it, taking it more seriously than when it was originally put forward, so that its full significance can be appreciated.[3]

Once a problem has been made, the process continues with defining and redefining the problem. Just as a storm comes into sharper focus from the conditions, content, and forces that formed it, a problem is articulated and sets the creative process into play. Defining becomes a general description of something specific. What does it include? What is not included? Who is involved? When? Where? Why? How? These questions have the form you give to them; the point is to define and redefine and redefine again so no questions are given preconceived answers. This includes a conscious framing of the problem.

FRAMING A PROBLEM

Gell-Mann writes that problem formulation involves finding the true boundaries of a problem. Problem making is another way of saying problem formulation. The true boundaries of a problem should set its frame. In his book, in the chapter "From Learning to Creative Thinking," Gell-Mann offers a famous brainteaser as an example.

As a child, I loved doing brainteasers, and I remember doing this one. The objective is to connect all nine dots by drawing, using four straight lines and not lifting the pencil from the paper. Most people assume that the solution lies in staying within the "box" made by the nine-dot grid. But that is not a stated constraint of the problem. In fact, you can solve the puzzle only by drawing lines outside the confines of the square area defined by the dots.

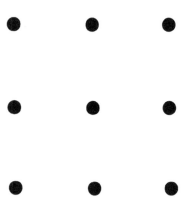

This is a literal illustration of "thinking outside the box." In a similar way, if the framing of the problem is too narrow, you've restricted what is included as room for possible solutions. If it is too vast, it tends to be unfocused and ill defined.

Many problems, of course, come in the form of statements already made by others, based on needs they have themselves defined. Even so, a creative practice requires the space made through questioning assumptions and preconceptions. From there, the impulse to know can fuel the creative process by making the problem felt and owned, again.

Consider this problem given to an architect: "put a window here." The architect unlearns, redefining the problem. It becomes something dramatically different when the preconceptions are eradicated from the architect's mind, which opens up the possibility for something new that is not based on preconceptions. The redefined problem is: "an aperture is needed for light, air, and view."

Whether a problem is first made on your own or you are given a problem that you redefine, you always end up as the creator if the impulse to know is something you yourself possess. Problem defining sets in motion the content and intention of how the problem will be solved. And that is why the way in which a problem is defined and framed will influence its course.

Problem defining is essential to problem solving because the definition of a problem sets in play the direction and momentum of its solution. It is important that a problem not be defined too narrowly, so that you can recognize potential discoveries along the way. Be wary of new assumptions regarding which ideas fit and don't fit along the path to a solution. Discoveries aren't always what we are looking for. The British who were digging up the rocks on the ocean floor were not seeking an explanation for continental drift.

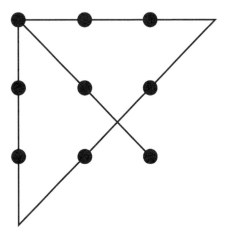

Looking for something you define too specifically may prevent you from seeing discoveries that are not exactly what you think you are trying to find. There may be no better example of this than the experience of the great American theoretical physicist Richard Feynman (1918–1988), who shared the 1965 Nobel Prize in Physics. He tells a story about how he came to make the discovery that won him that prize. It happened while he was at Cornell University.

I was in the cafeteria and some guy, fooling around, throws a plate in the air. As the plate went up in the air I saw it wobble, and I noticed the red medallion of Cornell on the plate going around. It was pretty obvious to me that the medallion went around faster than the wobbling. I had nothing to do, so I start figuring out the motion of the rotating plate. I discovered that when the angle is very slight, the medallion rotates twice as fast as the wobble rate—two to one. It came out of a complicated equation! I went on to work out equations for wobbles. Then I thought about how the electron orbits start to move in relativity. Then there's the Dirac equation in electrodynamics. And then quantum electrodynamics. And before I knew it ... the whole business that I got the Nobel Prize for came from that piddling around with the wobbling plate.[4]

A replica of the Cornell plate is now part of an exhibit celebrating the centennial of the Nobel Prize.

PROBLEM LIMITS

Understanding limits is important in defining the problem. Limits are what can and cannot be done, but they are often set based on preconceptions. For example, Gothic architecture would never have happened without discarding preconceived notions of what could and could not be done with stone. Stone is a pretty limited material; it works in compression. It doesn't work as well in tension or shear. So that means stones can be placed on stones; they can be piled up. They work most efficiently in compression. Gothic architects figured out that if the stone is placed along the path of stress or, in other words, the vector along which its load will be carried down the path of gravity to the ground, it can be piled high and span space.

This core principle of Gothic architecture is what Gaudí returned to when given the problem of finishing Sagrada Família, the Gothic cathedral. Rather than continuing based on Gothic style, he asked a question about the stylistic elements. Stylistic elements are often employed automatically, without connection to their purpose or principles. On examination, Gaudí could see the principles that

43

brought about the great inventions of Gothic architecture and started up, working from there. You could say that he rediscovered the impulse of Gothic structure. He based his design on the path of stress, along the vector that carries the stones' load down the path of gravity to the ground. How he did this is part of propelling, another element of the creative process.

Of course, not all limits can be traversed; understanding them is the key to being able to respond to them. You must understand that they have power, and responding to them requires some agility. In my observation of creative practice, you are in a good place if you can name the limits as a set of interactive variables. In architecture, engineering, and other disciplines, these variables lead to the design specifications, or "specs." The specifications, written or drawn, define by name, location, material, dimensions, and other facets what constitutes the design. They are part of all creative practice, even if "pure" artists would have you believe otherwise. Yes, the painter never has to specify "use 0.2 ounces of cyan 1.15 inches below and 2.68 feet to the right of the upper left corner," as the architect might stipulate regarding something in a measured drawing. Nor does the poet stipulate a tolerance for a phrase as an engineer might stipulate a tolerance for the turbine turning in a motor. Nevertheless, the painter and poet are doing this as part of refining their creative work.

Seeing how limits are interconnected also is key to being responsive. For example, weight and strength are connected. If the strength of something limits the weight it can carry, adding weight will require adding strength. Increasing the strength of a structure often means more structure, which is in itself additional weight. If time costs money and it takes longer to do B than A, opting for

B will require overcoming the limit of a budget set to the preconceived A.

The concept of *optimization* that is utilized by designers and engineers is based on defining the interrelationships of limits and overcoming constraints. It is a specific, frequently quantifiable outcome that is targeted. This is not disconnected from the authentic intention that forms out of the problem making from which all creative endeavors start.

CRAFTING PROBLEMS

Crafting problem statements is something I take seriously. I have conceived, written, and taught the first semester design curriculum for both graduate and undergraduate architecture students at RISD since 1992. Because this class has multiple sections, sometimes taught by faculty unfamiliar with our curriculum, the problem statements are the consistent vehicles for inducing learning. The problem needs to induce unlearning, as mentioned in chapter 2. I accomplish this in part by giving the students a problem both unfamiliar and daunting. The problem also needs to be written so the process of perceiving and conceiving (as discussed in chapter 6) are at work simultaneously; this helps ensure that the students don't get stuck in their heads or act mindlessly.

Whereas graduate students in this class tend to over conceptualize, the undergraduate students have a wonderful improvisational way of working, but have greater difficulty conceptualizing what they are doing. The problem needs to be written so the students each develop their own language while learning the basic conventions of architectural language. It needs to set up a process of the student's own gathering and tracking (as discussed in chapter 4) that launches the reiterative process.

The problem is a focused task students can start working on immediately. It has clear quantitative limits. I am careful to write these problems so they do not leave an indelible mark on each individual's development. I withhold from coloring the problem with any formal, stylistic, or theoretical bias. Meaning is something individuals find and define for themselves.

SUCCESSFUL PROBLEM MAKING

How do you know when your problem making is successful? The answer is that you have made an idea that moves you forward, that compels you to take the next step of gathering some intelligence (the subject of chapter 4). But you can get stuck in problem making if you think too much. My observation is that successful problem making is truly making, not just thinking—thought and action together.

Storm's-eye view 4.

GATHERING AND TRACKING

The problem making discussed in chapter 3 compels problem solving, which begins with gathering. You gather to refill the open space once occupied by our preconceptions. What I am calling *gathering* is known as different things in different practices: *collecting evidence* to a detective, *staging* for a contractor, *field studies* for a geologist, *evaluation* for a doctor, *foraging* or *procuring* for a chef, *jotting* for a poet, *research* for a scientist, and *sketching* for an artist. Evidence, equipment, rocks, tests, ingredients, associations, data, and images are collected. It may seem a benign activity, but it is not. It is full of potency. Gathering begins the process of acquiring, thereby structuring information, material, thought, and observations.

You may be free to start the gathering process as you wish or be given a protocol from which to work. It may happen gradually and organically. It may require the consistent following of a protocol or method; sometimes, though, the protocol or method may not be specifically tailored to a given situation.

The term *white-coat syndrome* refers to your elevated blood pressure reading because you're stressed by being examined by the doctor. The fact that this has been identified as a problem by name is a recognition of how a simple test meant to gather information might give misleading information. In this case, the identification led to a change in the protocol so it would be tailored to what is really going on. You may take note of these "exceptions" or modify how the gathering process is done. How that protocol or method was developed is itself a creative act. Sometimes you need to adopt the protocol or improvise. The point, again, is that gathering is potent.

I asked my good friend Frank Wilson about gathering. He is an internationally renowned neurologist and authority who has invested a lifetime in studying the hand, its relationship to the brain, and the neurological basis of skilled hand use. His book on the hand was even nominated for a Pulitzer Prize for nonfiction.[1]

Frank is critical of the presumptions that have accompanied the new emphasis on data collection and analysis, as if it is a comprehensive evaluation method for making a medical diagnosis. He told me about how framing a problem, which I discussed in chapter 3, establishes where the information for an evaluation will be gathered. Although the work of a detective and physician seem different, what Frank describes is much like establishing the perimeter at a crime scene using the ubiquitous yellow tape.

Another issue I think about a lot is how profoundly "framing" an interaction in medicine influences the interchange between doctors and patients. Younger doctors have absolutely no clue how much people know about their own problems and how much they withhold simply because they don't trust the person they've "hired." I always knew this was true (my dad was a small town GP and I loved listening to his stories), but it wasn't until I started practicing hand-reading on my patients (which happened because of the book I was working on). I very quickly learned that simply by pointing to something in the hand and talking about what hand-readers thought about it that a patient would literally commence a "dump" of personal information that I'd never have been given had I asked about it directly.

> If you want to find out about married life and stress, that's the last thing you want to ask about.... [J]ust point to the heart line and say that it has to do with emotions. Then stand back.[2]

I find the way artists and designers gather to be important in keeping an open mind and achieving an authentic creative work. Often it is done in an uncontrived way—meaning the creator is doing it sensibly, without concern for the creative work this activity is already imprinting. In my mind, how all the stuff (thoughts included) is being held together is already, at this stage, encoding the developing creative work.

At the outset of a project, you as the author of the work may not yet be able to speak about the final form of the creative activity or even direction you plan on taking it. But how the beginning observations and materials are related at the outset of a project is the seed of the project. Others of you may collect and gather obsessively, designing your own gathering as an instrument for recording a large amount of information.

Because there is no real protocol governing the way artists gather or research, the range of how gathering happens in creative practice is vast in the arts. For example, the infographics designer Nick Felton has made a creative practice of recording "random" aspects of his life. He has taken this practice into designing ways of recording data and has created apps that help. He creates what he calls "annual reports" of the information he collects about himself over the course of a year. His work caught the interest of Facebook, and he was invited to be a Facebook designer. It's his "timeline" concept that you now see on your Facebook page.[3]

GATHERED OBJECTS

As an architect, I place tremendous importance on how things are structured and held together. I read the thinking behind things in how they are held together. That is why I see this element of the creative process as so important. I often assign students who are about to begin their architectural theses projects to make a *gathered object*, meaning something that holds itself with no fasteners but by its own forces that define it. The tectonic order of the objects the students make can act as a kind of diagram of their thinking and launch their projects intelligently. In other words, how part relates to part in holding itself together can be an articulate diagram of the intentions of the project.

Gathered gravity suit.

I find it inspiring to look at examples of what I call gathered objects. A ball of string is a simple, elegant example. What we call it is also its structure. We don't call it string, but a ball of string. A ball of string is wound on a ball winder—a simple device with a shaft that is inclined on an angle as it rotates and gathers up the string. The spinning, inclined shaft causes the string to be wound on a precise spiral of great circles, which simultaneously builds up the ball and holds the previous loops on. As the diameter of the ball grows, an elegant structure of layered spirals holds the ball together. And that's it: the material arranged in an elegant geometry holds it together efficiently.

A storm is another, more complex example of a gathered object. It is an extensive gathering of moisture, heat, and particles, pushed and pulled by itself, gathering the air over stretches of ocean and continent. A storm forms from indistinguishable things and conditions. It may begin from a little disturbance that is fueled by warm water. Water molecules in warm waters collide, and some of these colliding molecules escape the ocean and become water vapor. The vapor rises because warm air rises from the source to the sink of the cooler air above, losing the heat as it rises and condensing into droplets.

As the storm grows, it becomes better organized; it creates a kind of little engine that converts heat energy into the mechanical energy of the winds that power it. Storms have behaviors, momentum, direction, and produce significant consequences. It structures itself, pulling material from all around to become its own structure distinct from other weather systems. The "gathering storm" is a great analogy for the creative process.

A flock of birds is another gathered object. Anyone who has seen a flock of starlings, called a murmuration, has been struck by the magic with which they gather and shift and move. It seems so coherent and adaptive. The cloud of birds looks like a translucent flag. A group of Princeton University engineers that teamed up with a couple of Italian physicists to better understand how a murmuration works called it "a formation of iron filings guided by an invisible magnet in the sky."[4]

Two of the physicists, from the Sapienza Unit of the Institute for Complex Systems (ISC-CNR) in Rome, had found that each bird keeps track of only seven other birds out of the thousands in the flock; these are the seven closest neighbors. Two Princeton

Murmuration of starlings.

engineers used videos shot by the Italians to create a mathematical model that allowed them to evaluate the coordination and consensus needed in the flock, and create a kind of cost-benefit model. The engineers found that when each bird tracks seven neighbors, this is the most efficient use of energy given the uncertainty of the situation. They also found that the flock is shaped more like an undulating "fluffy pancake" than like a sphere or egg. This thinner, undulating shape allows the birds to keep track of the seven neighbors and hold together, while also encountering many uncertain and unpredictable conditions and changes.

Wouldn't it be great to have such an adaptive, coherent structure for dwelling in the uncertainty of the creative process?

By comparing the order of gathering in each of these examples, a distinctly different order becomes apparent for each that functions and has a geometry specific to it. What I mean by order is the abstract organization that holds the whole together. That is what gives it an overall form. I see the gathering and ungathering whenever I observe creative practice, or engage in it myself.

INTELLIGENCE

I give these examples to inspire a creative conscious gathering. It is influenced by how the problem is defined and framed. It is influenced by the content of what you gather. The way you gather begins to structure or hold together content, and begins to structure or give form to an idea. This gathering structure is the genetic code of form. This form giving is intelligence: "I gather that ... " (a phrase that persists in colloquial usage). By intelligence I mean how we take information in, process it, and project it back out.

When you gather, you become your own search engine. In a 2004 interview, Sergey Brin, one of the founders of Google, said, "Certainly if you had all the world's information directly attached to your brain, or an artificial brain that was smarter than your brain, you'd be better off." This, he explained, was why he and his cofounder, Larry Page, aspired to make Google a "perfect search engine that could understand exactly what you mean and gives you back exactly what you want."[5]

Theirs was a great ambition for the advancement of access to information, but only you as your own search engine can find answers to questions like these: How do I know what to do? Where to go? When it's right? This is why you gather as part of the creative process. You are making something of nothing, sense out of nonsense. You are finding your own way. The gathering itself happens through the senses, through the eyes, hands, ears, and so on. It happens in the form of perception (see chapter 6). By gathering, you bring together to discern. You gather to speak and reason through words. You gather to know. You gather to find the connections between things from part to part and part to whole.

Related colloquial expressions reveal that there are many "ways of knowing," each used interchangeably with "I know": I reckon; I get it; I grasp it; I figure; I see.

It is interesting to think about what you are saying when you use these expressions. *Reckoning* has to do with *counting*. From there, you get to *recounting*, which means to tell a story. These are gathering through numbers or words. *I got it* is stating that you possess what is needed to know or understand. *I grasp it* speaks more specifically to your hand's way of knowing, although it is used more generally. *Figuring* has to do with shaping or giving form to something—a coming into being through form. *I see* expresses perception as the vehicle for knowing.

Let's look at the etymology of *intelligence*, and words used to define its meaning. The meaning of the word intelligence seems to have two aspects. One meaning is "perception," which comes from the Latin word *percipere*: to take hold of, or to feel. The other is "discernment," which comes from *discernere*, a Latin word that combines *dis* (apart) and *cernere* (to separate). Our English word *certain* is rooted in the Latin word *certus*, which was a form of cernere meaning "determined" or "fixed."

That is about the words used to define our word intelligence, but what about the word itself? It comes from the Latin words *inter*, meaning "among," and *legere*, meaning "to gather." Hence, gathering.

We gather because our cleared minds need to be filled, and the gathering is how we commence solving the problem of that absence created by losing our preconceptions.

Ultimately, intelligence is imprinted in what we create/make; it is like the fundamental code, the DNA of your creative practice. A creative work is a condensation of its making. What you put into it stays there and speaks for you.

Different ways of knowing (of figuring, seeing, grasping, taking in information) imprints traits on what we do, say, and make. The way you gather starts to structure or hold together content, and starts to structure or give form to an idea. This gathering structure is the genetic code of form; it is the form that the creative work takes.

Any great work of architecture has been built from a consistent DNA: how parts relate to parts, and how parts relate to the whole.

This is the tectonic order (discussed in chapter 5). In looking at the work of the great Finnish architect and designer Alvar Aalto (1898–1976), you can see the geometry of bent laminated wood in the details, but also in the overall spatial organization. The plan of his Baker House, a dormitory at MIT in Cambridge, Massachusetts, is arranged as a curved layered bar with functions. *Bar* and *bar building* are terms that architects use to refer to long, rectangular blocks of buildings. A bar building has its longitudinal dimension in the horizontal orientation, whereas a tower has it longitudinal dimension in the vertical orientation. The dorm rooms that comprise the curved bar building have the geometry of a straight layered bar that was laterally divided and *then* curved. This is a different geometry than a curved bar that is laterally divided *after* it was curved. These geometric traits in the building's design came from a generative process of working with material that was layered and bent. In fact, Aalto made many studies of bent plywood for the furniture he designed. The divisions of the bar of the dormitory were inherent in its form from the start. The divisions were to become the rooms for the community of students. The consequence of this subtle but significant difference in geometry affects the experience of the rooms, views from the rooms, and way in which the windows and brickwork of the curved facade is detailed. Instead of cookie-cutter rooms made by slicing the curved dormitory bar, each individual room is part of the initial diagram that was shaped, making the dormitory a community of individuals.

There are countless examples of how beginning studies imprint the final architecture. Gaudí's design of the Sagrada Família, which I detail in chapter 5, is dependent on the fact that he "sketched" his thoughts in three dimensions using ropes and weights. This was a

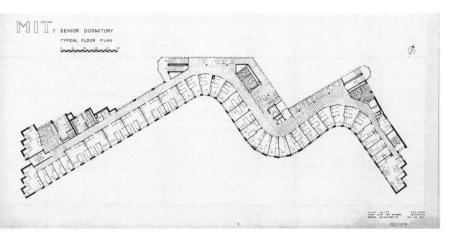

Plan of Baker House.

distinctive way of gathering those thoughts and ideas about structure, form, program … everything.

Consider knots, which are gathered objects. One knot can be so different from another. They are the results of what formed them. A sailor's knot is designed as a direct response to its purpose. There are also all the knots that happen by chance, from a tangle in a little girl's hair, to a necklace chain, to thread you put away without winding and securing it on its spool. There are also mathematical knots. All three types have a specific configuration of gathering and ungathering. One depends on a choreographed gesture, another on an occurrence of consequence built on chance, and yet another on its mathematical definition. The specific organization of the material or ideas that are gathered influences and imprints traits into the developing solution. Again, this is not a benign activity but instead plays a determining role in what is to come.

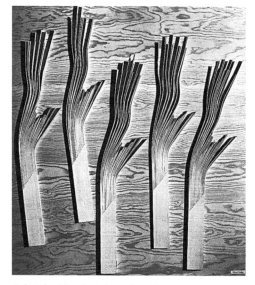

Aalto's bent laminated wood studies.

TRACKING

Out of gathering emerges the ideal or goal, the beginning of defining what will ultimately be created. You get the "traits" that need to be tracked. It is like the gathering of data points to display on an x-y axis: the line that emerges from those points becomes the ideal. In the creative process, it is the early indication of what will ultimately be created.

You see this played out in the pharmaceutical development process. The scientist takes data and uses them to plot a graph. The placement of the data points along a graph with an x-axis, and a y-axis reveals to the scientist the direction to follow. Soon, the characteristics of the drug that will ultimately be created are revealed.

In any general case, as in the example of the drug, the ideal or goal comes from the structure of how the gathered content is held together. It is specific and fleeting, like the scent we need to follow or track. We go from gathering with our newly opened minds to tracking, which involves a purposeful pursuit that is gaining clarity.

Tracking, is the gerund of the verb *track* and means to follow a particular course, as in the transitive—"meteorologists are tracking the storm"—as well as intransitive use—"the storm is tracking across the ground at thirty miles per hour. Track means "to follow the traces of" and is associated etymologically with *tract,* which comes from the Latin root *trahere,* the past participle of *tractus,* the action of drawing (along) and act of drawing. The words track, tract, trait, and trace all relate to drawing—which is how I understand the role of drawing—as a verb. The French word *trait* is used to refer to an act of drawing, specifically "a stroke in the delineation of character." It is a process of tracking, a dynamic pursuit that is continually being updated through the feedback that is drawn up. It clarifies and guides us to make editorial decisions.

The painter Alfred DeCredico (1944–2009) taught drawing as a foundations professor at RISD. Even when creating eight-foot-wide oil paintings, some of which had fur, bones, and electric lamps as part of their composition, he understood that drawing was the primary process in creating the painting. For DeCredico,

DRAWING is a solitary activity during which the artist engages in the act of creating, not replicating, an experience. IT has the capacity for relevance beyond "aesthetic"—can not distinguish between the painter or the architect, the sculptor or the designer of objects. IT allows for existence in a place of possibility, between the present and the future, where "knowing" and "discovery" collide and merge.[6]

Tracking involves oscillating about an abstraction. *Abstraction* means to draw away from (*ab* = away from + *tract* = draw). The abstract ideal or goal is pulled away from, distinguished from the clutter of all the context of the problem. The periodic oscillation in the feedback control function of a thermostat is an example of tracking. It becomes the standard for the form, which is the "definiteness" of the idea or goal. It also begins to define the more precise relationship of the limits I introduced in chapter 3.

The idea of a search with feedback, an oscillation around an "intended" outcome, is analogous to the reiterative cycle of projecting/making/feedback/reflection/critique of creative practice. This cycle depends on traits identified through gathering that define tracking, which in turn leads to more specific gathering. Tracking and gathering are interdependent. It is tracking that holds the murmuration together, and it is the collective intelligence or gathering of the flock that enables it to track the sky. This reiterative process is an oscillation of author, work, world, and intention. It simultaneously absorbs, propels, corrects, and posits.

By tracking, in this context, I mean the reiterative and oscillating cycles of pursuit and honing in with the mind, like a direct grasp of intuition of the other. The sensation is a clearly possessed sense of purpose often accompanied with the thought "I don't know what I am doing but I know I have to do this." DeCredico tracks his process without any a priori destination. "DRAWING is exploration and adventure. I draw a drawing until I am shocked by what the drawing tells me and I find myself in a place where I have never been before. I begin a drawing not knowing where I am going and end it when the drawing tells me that I've gotten there."

I think there are ostensible intentions, initiating intentions and the real intention of the work itself. Ostensible intention may be the intention implied by a given problem before it was questioned, along with all its preconceptions. Initiating intention is what emerges as unlearning takes place. The real intention of a work develops as the abstract generative process takes hold.

It is important to distinguish the real developing purpose of the work itself from the author of the work's ego-invested insistent stubbornness of preconceptions masquerading as intentions.

Hugo, the poet and creative writing teacher, used the terms *initiating* or *triggering subject* versus the real or generative subject:

> A poem can be said to have two subjects, the initiating or triggering subject, which starts the poem or "causes" the poem to be written, and the real or generated subject, which the poem comes to say or mean, and which is generated or discovered in the poem during the writing. That's not quite right because it suggests that the poet recognizes the real subject. The poet may not be aware of what the real subject is but only have some instinctive feeling that the poem is done.[7]

Tracking is also the way in which you begin to see the tolerance associated with the idea or goal. For example, if you are creating a map, the weight of the lines on the map will depend on the overall size of the map. At some point, a line would simply be too heavy to function on a given map; a thick line on a small map would render the map unreadable. A fat line drawn on a map of a certain scale, designating borders between nations, could represent ten kilometers in reality. That brings the concept of tolerance home.

Tolerance, the allowable oscillation around the standard or goal within the relationships between limits, can be found in several ways. One is through play. That is how the dimensions of a baseball diamond came to be set. The distance between bases and the distance from the pitcher's mound to home plate reflect the tolerance for human activity specific to the game and within the creation of baseball. Those dimensions were arrived at through trial and error, or through the play of the variables, which were influenced by the athleticism of pitching, batting, running, catching, stealing, throwing, sliding, tagging, and so on. They have to do with equipment-enhancing abilities. And they have to do with immeasurable aspects such as human will, motivation, and other human attributes.

All these variables come down to and are held in balance by the dimensions of the baseball diamond. It keeps the ability of the team at bat in balance or *at play* with the abilities of the team on the field. If the bases were farther apart, for instance, players wouldn't make it to the bases fast enough, and there would be three outs before anyone made it all the way around the bases to score a run. If the pitcher's mound was farther away from home plate, the hitter would have a greater advantage, advancing to first base on a walk or accumulating more hits because the ball would have slowed by the time it reached the plate, keeping the team at bat indefinitely as it accumulated runs. If the pitcher's mound was closer to home plate, there would be far fewer hits and more strikeouts, causing both teams to alternate over and over from offense to defense before any runs could be scored. The dimensions of the diamond weren't arrived at theoretically but instead empirically through play, through the playing out of the game with all its variables at play. It holds in balance the difficulty of being at bat or fielding a position.

Tolerances can also be found through procedure. Take the example of an algorithm, a step-by-step procedure for calculations based on a finite list of well-defined rules or instructions. The goal or idea is the output determined by executing those steps one after the other. But they are full of tolerances. In this case, the tolerances are different combinations of variables that have limits.

The third way is through permutations and a process of elimination. Parametrics, constants in equations that vary in other equations of the same general form, offer an extreme example of computational permutations to achieve a standard of limits, as in the design of an airplane's wings.

In creative practice, when you use materials to generate ideas, you anticipate tolerances and so have to use the right medium. The tolerance of milled steel is tighter than wood, for example. Ideas also have tolerances. Some ideas are tight, and others have a loose fit, with wide margins of error.

I designed a turned wooden bowl that amplified and celebrated tolerance. The design consisted of a simple specification: the outside was specified as a sphere of a certain dimension. The inside or interior space of the bowl was defined as an ellipsoid of specified major and minor axes. The relationship of the center of the sphere and center of the ellipsoid was defined and specified. The top edge of the bowl was a result of the three specifications, or where the ellipsoid and sphere intersected. This was a limited edition production by a fine Viennese wood turner. The geometry I specified was volatile. The slightest shift between the outer sphere and ellipsoid in the process of turning the bowl would bring out a dramatically different shape. The slightest shift between these two forms would alter the cross section and affect the way the bowl balances. As a result, no two bowls could be made exactly the same. They expressed the tolerance of the geometry and the tolerance of the craft of wood turning.

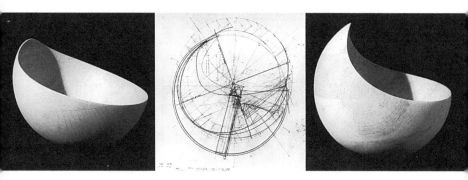

Two bowls made from the same specifications.

With your gathering and tracking undertaken, the creative process is empowered by purpose and intention. Best-selling author and speaker Deepak Chopra (b. 1947) writes of what he calls "The Law of Intention and Desire," one of seven "spiritual laws of success":

> Inherent in every intention and desire is the mechanics for its fulfillment.... [I]ntention and desire in the field of pure potentiality have infinite organizing power.
>
> And when we introduce an intention in the fertile ground of pure potentiality, we put this infinite organizing power to work for us....

This law is based on the fact that energy and information exist everywhere in nature. In fact, at the level of the quantum field, there is nothing other than energy and information. The quantum field is just another label for the field of pure consciousness or pure potentiality. And this quantum field is influenced by intention and desire.[8]

Like a storm that has gathered itself and is tracking as it gathers energy, the process enters a phase I have observed in creative practice that I call propelling.

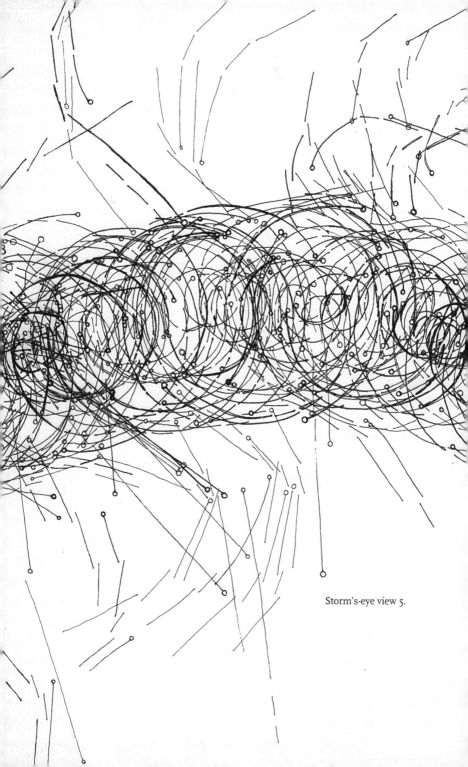

Storm's-eye view 5.

PROPELLING

Propelling is a property of the storm and also a property of the creative process. The storm is propelled forward by its own action, fueled by gathering and directed by tracking. What propels the creative process forward is also gathering and tracking, and the action of an evolving, organic language that is as old as the discipline that employs it. For a writer, that language is words. A musician's language is sounds and tones and timbres, often expressed with notation. Scientists often employ equations, which come from mathematics. Engineers have a structural language. Dancers "speak" in the language of movement.

Discipline-based languages have many layers or aspects. Some aspects are learned; they are based on conventions on which clear communication relies. People who use their hands in their work also develop a language; some aspects of the language may come from training (a woodworking intern learning to sharpen a chisel, for example), whereas others are developed, authored by individuals themselves as part of an internalized conversation aimed at clarifying the developing work and without concern about communicating with others. As a teacher and critic who needs to decipher and read the languages operating in a creative work, I know that even the internalized conversations made through the work are surprisingly and inherently legible.

Neurologist Frank R. Wilson tells a story about the communication among a surgical team during an operation on which he assisted as a resident. The team comprised five or six people, including an anesthesiologist, all dressed in long gowns and masks. The chief surgeon also wore a "modified snorkel apparatus" connected to a vacuum line to prevent his breath from contaminating the surgical site. For however long the surgery lasted, even six to ten hours, the chief surgeon would be so equipped and would have to stay put in the same spot.

Despite all of these peculiarities, to my mind none was quite so remarkable as the fact that, to the best of my recollection, this surgeon *never* spoke a word during any of his operations, nor did he permit anyone else to speak. Just for a moment, imagine yourself standing at this operating table, doing your part to assist through a long and difficult operation. How would you know what the surgeon was doing? How would you know what *you* were supposed to do, or when you were supposed to do it? I can tell you how it was done: everyone watched the surgeon's hands and what he was doing with the operating instruments. These were not naive observers. Their own professional knowledge of brain anatomy and surgical technique, their complete familiarity with the team strategy for removing tumors, and their instant grasp of the significance of every nuance of movement of the leader's arms, wrists, hands and fingers, made his assistants equal and fully informed participants in the ongoing and richly informative *but completely silent* conversation that began with the first touch of a scalpel to the patient's forehead and did not conclude until the last suture was securely in place many hours later.

What kind of language was this? I would be tempted to call it a San Francisco dialect of mainstream operative neurosurgical sign language. No one invented this language, named it, or even considered it to be a language as such. It just came into being in this particular community, where it thrived for a number of years and eventually became the principal operating room language of residents who trained on this particular team at this particular time. Its deep structure, its conjoined semantics and syntactics, were absolutely typical of every human language that has ever existed, whether spoken or signed, and its emergence can be understood as the natural outgrowth of shared expertise, cooperative labor, the association of skilled movement with complex knowledge and intentionality, and of the innate capacity of each individual initiated into the rituals of neurosurgical work to construct his or her own meaning from the signs being exchanged between those present.[1]

As you become literate in your discipline's language or the development of your own language, you are freed up to play with the language's logic. So a musician may play with the harmonic scale in music; the scientist may play with the laws of algebra in the unfolding of a physics equation; a writer may play with grammatical practices from language, and with how the meaning and usage of words has changed. Suspend control of meaning and concentrate on the language's pattern, and that kind of play generates momentum. It is like the poet who paints a sonic world of softness with particular sounds of the words she chooses to use in writing her poem. Relinquish a correspondence of cause and effect, or where the process will lead (intention), and unburden the play with language from solving a problem (purpose), and you generate further momentum. In other words, work with the language itself, not with what the language necessarily represents.

The propelling action of a storm is the cyclonic circulation in the atmosphere, called cyclogenesis. Once a cluster of thunderstorms in the tropics begins to organize and rotate around and about each other, a chain reaction can occur. The rotation rate of these thunderstorms' cyclonic action increases; they become more vigorous and unified as the wind increases. The clusters of thunderstorms become a tropical storm. Water molecules collide and rise out of the warm ocean as vapor and condense into droplets in the cool air above. The tropical storm's engine converts that heat energy from the condensed droplets into the mechanical energy of the winds and powers the storm. When the storm's winds reach around seventy miles per hour, an eye develops. The eye is surrounded by what is called an eye wall, which is an intense ring of heat and the strongest winds. The hurricane is propelled.

This momentum of play with language can be harnessed in the creative process, because language can carry more than what you intended. There are many embedded traits in language that carry more than just the "technical" meaning of word. Syllables are units of sound. Durations of a line of verse or sentence in prose can be measured as, and thus convey, breath. Scansion is rhythmic breathing. A dancer's movements may be triggered by the geometric logic of his choreography. An architect may follow the logic from the scale of how one material addresses another material to how two spaces intersect, abut, or stand apart.

Intelligent play with language carries more than what you intend, creating a momentum of ideas. I observe that in the creative process, playing and following the logic of the language, without concern for what something might end up being, propels the process forward. It is important periodically to take stock of where the play with language has taken you.

As the Swiss artist Klee wrote, "Drawing is taking a line for a walk."[2] In fact, like walking a dog, the line is just as likely to take you for a walk.

Play with language should be moderated by a kind of "what have I done?" evaluative check from time to time.

SYNTAX

Every language has syntax, the way in which its elements (e.g., words) are put together to form constituents (e.g., phrases or clauses). For example, tectonics is the syntax in the language of architecture. Tectonics governs the way in which elements are put together. It is the meeting points or joints at all scales, whether material to material, wall to wall, room to room, building to building, or building to environment. Tectonics is the meeting of different conditions: public to private, sacred to profane, light to shade, inside to outside, or blind spots to views. One could say that architecture establishes relations, and tectonics is the syntax of relations. It is how architects express; it is also how we put together thoughts and buildings.

The etymology of tectonics leads us to *tekne* and *text*. From tekne comes technique and technology. From *tekton* comes tectonic and architect. From *textus* is *texere*, or woven, text, textile, and context: a woven narrative. Thus, we find the relationship between tectonics and expression.

Material has properties and laws like a language. Material is a language for artists and designers. Material is a language for developing ideas; the material used in a process may not be the same as the material used in the final product.

A material's behavior "talks" back to you. There are material tolerances, and material complains if it is mistreated. The conversation between you and material disrupts the monologue of intentions the artist and designer has—that is, the conversation you have with yourself as part of creative practice, and into which no materials have yet been invited. Material doesn't always participate in the plans you have for it.

The artist's word for material is *medium*. The dictionary defines the word as something in a middle position, and also as a means of effecting or conveying something. To the artist, the medium goes between the preconceived and revealed idea. It transmits, just as a medium does so, serving as the "go-between" at a séance. It also can get in the way. When you let the materials at hand get in the way, you put yourself in a good position for discovery. Understood this way, medium opens the mind to discoveries.

MATERIAL AS LANGUAGE

Earlier, I wrote of the language employed by musicians, scientists, engineers, and dancers. For architects like myself, material is a generative language. It works just like the languages of those other disciplines. Within our language, there are material geometries or shapes that materials take when hung, bent, folded, crumpled, gathered, spun, and so on. The geometries or shapes are a result of the behavior and forces that manipulated the material.

The catenary curve is a good example of what I mean. It is the curve formed when a material that works in pure tension, is uniformly dense, and is inextensible, typically in the form of a cable or chain, is suspended from its endpoints. The curve that results replicates the graph of the function in trigonometry known as a hyperbolic cosine.

A catenary curve is an elegant form because there is only one catenary. Whether the endpoints are close or faraway, the same curve is produced—different segments of the same curve but at a different scale. If you hold a certain length of chain in your hands two feet apart, that catenary is the same catenary as if you hold that same length of chain in your hands but three feet apart. The difference is simply that the curve you see with your hands three feet apart is a magnification of the apparently steeper curve when your hands are closer together.

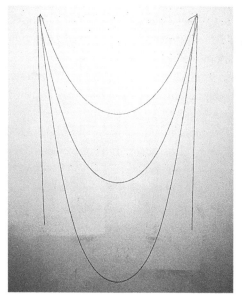

Catenary curve.

I introduced Gaudí in chapter 2, and discussed his work some more in chapter 3. Gaudí used material behavior, material geometry, material tolerances, and material analogies. His masterwork, Sagrada Família, demonstrates all these aspects of material reasoning in generating structural, formal, and spatial ideas as well as conceptualizing the order of the whole.

Recall that Sagrada Família actually began as a commission for Gaudí to finish a Gothic cathedral already under construction. It was started under the direction of a previous architect. The Gothic period was an amazing time in architecture, when stone was made to soar. As I wrote about in chapter 3, stone is a pretty limited material: it works in compression, but doesn't work well in tension or shear. So stones can be placed on stones; they can basically be piled up. Again, Gothic architects had figured out that stone placed along the stress path—that is, the vector along which its load will be carried down by gravity to the ground—could be piled higher and higher and higher, spanning space.

Gaudí looked into the principles of Gothic architecture and took things further. He based his design on the catenary curve. That curve exists by acting in pure tension. Make it rigid and inverted, and it would be in pure compression, like the famous Gateway Arch in Saint Louis, Missouri. Gaudí made models, funicular models, completely from catenary curves, from knotted cords and weights. He mentally inverted these models to envision the building. He used cord and weights to generate the form of the building—forms that are intelligent, structurally logical, and inventive. By strictly following the line of the catenary, the line of the stress, in the design and placement of the axes of the columns, he reduced the horizontal

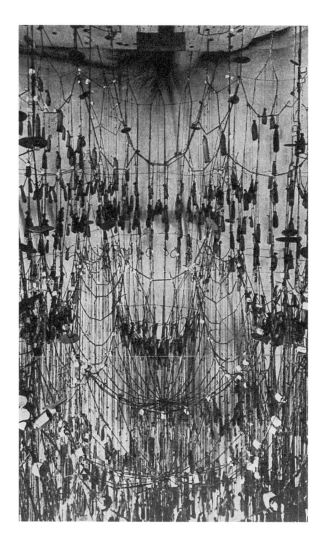

Gaudí's funicular model.

thrust and eliminated the need for the buttresses that are a feature of most cathedrals.

The flying buttress was used to counteract the tremendous thrust in the tall vaults typical in Gothic architecture. Gaudí's central spanning vault, while matching and surpassing the heights of most Gothic cathedrals, requires no buttress, because the thrust was minimized and carried within the lines of the structure of the central span itself. He invented the tilted columns that carry the thrust of the church's central nave. By tilting the columns along the line of stress, the stress is internalized within the columns' mass, requiring no buttressing. These columns are articulated beautifully following the geometric logic of drapery. Gaudí arrived at this geometry by hanging, tying, and stressing cloth. While the geometry he developed is new, its undulations refer to the fluted columns used since classic architecture.

Gaudí's funicular models are not only complex models of structure, spatial organization, geometry, and program. Gaudí was a spiritual man. He used his funicular models as a way of modeling analogously. The gravity that shaped the catenary curves in the models, when inverted conceptually, shaped the stone. In essence, by sketching his ideas using gravity, he represented, when inverted, the force of the heavens, shaping the church.

PROPELLED TO PERCEPTION AND CONCEPTION

As with a storm, this propelling in creative practice is leading somewhere. It is taking you to a phase during which you will be shifting from the abstract to the concrete (and from the concrete workings to their abstractions), leading forward to the creation of something real that represents the goal/ideal I wrote of earlier. It is a cyclic process, not linear, which may take you back to other phases I've already written about, to gather more material and track the course of momentum.

In chapter 6, I introduce perception, which leads to conception and propels the process forward even more. The modernist American poet Charles Olson understood how this works. He wrote in his manifesto "Projective Verse" of "the process of the thing, how the principle can be made so to shape the energies that the form is accomplished. And I think it can be boiled down to one statement (first pounded into my head by Edward Dahlberg): 'One perception must immediately and directly lead to a further perception.'"[3]

As with the storm propelled, you are now propelled to perceiving and conceiving.

Storm's-eye view 6.

PERCEIVING AND CONCEIVING

Sensibility is an intimately felt knowledge that hinges on perception. It may include everything from how you process a simple technical task to how you position an observation you make in a broader context of the world. It is based, though, on something felt and on knowledge you actually absorb in your body. Sensibility is not just how you take in information through your sensory organs. It is also about how you use that information to form a concept that places you in relation to the world. It is an element of the creative process.

I can still recall an experience of sensibility I had as a child. I put a key into a lock, but the key stuck. There was some desperation as I tried hard to turn the key, but it just wouldn't budge. I tried again and again, and then I thought I felt the key bend inside the lock.

At that moment, though, there was no way I could tell for certain whether the key had actually bent. It was stuck, and there was nothing to see. But I had felt the soft, slow movement of folding metal.

This was a turning point for me: feeling something, not quite knowing how I had felt it, not knowing whether what I felt had really happened, and doubting my own perception. I yanked on the key again, and it broke off in the lock. It was one of my first conscious lessons in sensibility.

Perceiving is what happens in the creative process as gathering and tracking continue and become more effective and purposeful. Gathering through the senses feeds your perception and thus your sensibility. It creates a unique point of view, a way of knowing that is yours but that can be connected to a more universal point of view.

"COME TO YOUR SENSES"

You can look at the storm from different scales and different points of view, and see things differently. If you look from the mesoscale of a tropical storm, you can see the cyclogenesis at work, forming and intensifying until the storm has rain bands, an eye, and an eyewall. There are distinct features defined by their boundaries.

If you look at the internal workings of a storm from the point of view of a water molecule, however, you see something different. The water molecule goes on an extensive and transformative journey. It leaves the ocean, encounters the air, and warms up and cools down, experiencing countless collisions, rising in a cyclone and then falling as rain. The line drawn between the storm's features is not just porous but also in constant flux. Vapor is becoming liquid, and liquid is becoming vapor continuously, but at a rate so constant that macroscopically, the entities are stable.

The molecular scale of the storm is analogous to the flow of the point of view through sensibility. Our perception extends outward and inward, extending our grasp of the world. We encounter different conditions, experiencing and moving through them, and they transform us.

The Hungarian British author Arthur Koestler is probably best known for his 1940 antitotalitarian novel *Darkness at Noon*, but he also wrote extensively about creativity, changing scientific paradigms, and culture broadly. He drew a similar metaphoric connection between perception as water, calling the world of perception "aquatic"—in which "the organism [is] submerged in a fluid environment of sounds, shapes, and smells." He described conceptualized thought as "dry and inexhaustible, like the atmosphere," and stated that the "highest forms of purely perceptual abstraction on the pre-verbal level are like bubbles of air which aquatic creatures extract from the water."[1] This is what I refer to as sensibility: conceptualized thought extracted through perception.

Let me try to explain. Many years after the incident with the key in the lock, when I was an undergraduate architecture student at The Cooper Union in New York City, a shop technician by the name of Max Hyder was teaching me how to use a band saw, a power tool that includes a table on which you rest the material to be cut. You feed the material through a blade that is constantly sliding in a downward direction. The act of feeding the material to the blade is not unlike working with a sewing machine. Typically, you or someone else has marked the material with a line so you know where to cut. Also typically, you know which side of the line is the material that will be shaped and saved, and which side will be discarded.

"If you think you are off, you are." The maxim was central to Hyder's lesson.

I started my first cut, and sure enough, although I could not yet see that I was off the line, I felt I was. But I doubted myself, and continued, which took me even farther off the line. The next time it happened, I trusted the sense I had and backed off the blade.

Sensing you are "off the mark" before you can confirm it visually is a prime example of your perception informing awareness that leads to sensibility.

Let me give you another example. If you've been in the stands at a baseball game, you've seen outfielders run to catch fly balls. From your vantage point, their paths can seem mystifying. Sometimes they run backward, then forward, then to the left, and then to the right, speeding up and slowing down, and then perhaps retracing some of their own steps. It looks erratic. If you were to try plotting it, it would prove quite complex. If a GoPro camera were mounted on an outfielder's head, though, it would capture what actually appears to be a surprisingly elegant motion.

Two Dutch scientists use the theory of optical acceleration cancellation (OAC) to explain how outfielders in baseball position themselves on the field to catch fly balls.[2] The scientists were seeking an interception theory to explain a "catcher standing in the plane of motion of the ball" and determined that OAC was the only one that works. (Other researchers have used OAC to examine how soccer players head the ball.) Basically, the Dutch scientists' argument goes like this. The ball accelerates from the impact with the bat, spins, lifts in the arc of its trajectory, then decelerates as air resistance and gravity begin to take over, and finally turns. Players position themselves so the ball appears to be moving straight at them at a constant rate. At the same time, the players move depending on their location on the field. Their movement may be any of the directions you see from the stands. Their objective at every moment is to keep the ball appearing, from their unique perspective, to be moving in a straight line and at a constant speed.

The OAC and outfielder is a simple example of how your point of view is unique, distinct, unlike that of anyone else. It shows the outfielder's own sensibility. Each of us has our own sensibility. In creative practice, sensibility is the bridge between perceiving and conceiving.

Sensibility, which involves a back-and-forth between perception and concept, is familiar to the artist. When you draw from life, you are constantly conversing back and forth between what you see or sense and how you conceptualize these in the form of the drawing. For instance, imagine drawing a bowl of fruit. Your eye is focused on the curved edge of the bowl's top, and your hand gets into motion, perhaps with a gesture that describes the curve of the bowl's top edge as your eye traces its three-dimensional arc. In this example, you're feeling and seeing at the same time. Those two senses are linked. Perhaps it begins simply as a notion of roundness, and then perhaps becomes something else. The conception is playing out in the process of observation and drawing.

In actuality, the bowl's edge is a circle that is tilted relative to your viewing plane, and so it is perceived as elliptical. Knowing this perspectival concept affects how your drawing hand moves. Everything is locked into the spatial matrix that is felt, seen, and a conceptual placement in the world. You draw the arc of the bowl's top edge by sensing and comparing the drawn gesture to the appearance of the bowl's edge, and through conceptualizing what is being drawn. Layers of perception and concept reverberate until you know what to add, what to change, what to erase, and what feels right, until you're satisfied with the view of the world your drawing creates.

I've participated in wine tastings that work in a similar way, going from the perceptual to conceptual. First, we are presented with several uncorked bottles of wine, each with its identity masked. Next we each take a sip, and are invited to grunt and express what we taste. Then the wine expert asks questions that give us ways to be inquisitive about what we hesitantly taste, smell, and see. So, for example, if someone says a wine tastes "dusty," the expert might ask, "Dusty like the basement or attic?"

When our descriptions are precise enough, the expert substantiates what we've sensed by describing the conditions under which the grapes were grown. He might tell us they come from the north side of a hill in Umbria, were grown in cool, indirect light, and that the hillside was well drained and had rocky, mineral-rich soil. These, he explains, conspire in the fermenting process to create the subtle chemical and material differences we identify through our senses of taste, mouthfeel, and smell.

The expert gives a wonderful tour, guided by our sensibility from the phenomenal to noumenal (as I discussed in chapter 1), and from a glass of wine to culture and place. His feedback, as in any creative practice, allows us to employ our perceptions to move forward to conception.

Michael Grab, an artist born in Edmonton, Alberta, who now works in Boulder, Colorado, has been creating rock-balancing art for nearly a decade. He relies on sensibility for the duration of making one of his pieces. Grab balances rocks on top of each other in precarious states. His description of his process includes what he sees, feels, and hears (perception) as well as a conceptualization of resolving vectors of forces in creating equilibrium.

Balance requires a minimum of THREE contact points. Luckily, every rock is covered in a variety of tiny to large indentations that can act as a NATURAL TRIPOD for the rock to stand upright, or in most orientations you can think of with other rocks. By paying close attention to the vibrations of the rocks, you will start to feel even the smallest "clicks" as the notches of the rocks are moving over one another. In the finest "point-balances," these clicks can be felt on a scale smaller than millimeters, and in rare cases can even go undetected, in which case intuition and experience become quite useful. Some point-balances will give the illusion of weightlessness as the rocks look to be barely touching. But if you look very close, you may be able to see the tiny notches in which the rocks rest.

Woven through the physical element of finding tripods, the most fundamental non-physical element is likened to meditation; finding a zero point or silence within myself. Some balances can apply significant pressure on the rational mind and patience. One of the great challenges is to overcome any doubt that may arise. To consider that seemingly impossible things may just be possible. Sometimes I don't even feel the vertices of the finest "tripods" or balance points until I've spent enough time slowing down to the related threshold of vibrations.[3]

On his Web site, you can see some of Grab's pieces being made from the point of view of a video camera worn on his head (http://www.gravityglue.com/portfolio/counter-point-balance).

Nicholas Evans-Cato (b. 1973) is a painter and colleague of mine at RISD, where he teaches in foundation studies. He painted the tree below while teaching in Jerusalem. The next day he saw an actual explosion that made him realize a tree is an explosion, too. It just happens over a much greater period than what he saw that day. You don't see the tree explode because it is outside an observable time frame, unless a representation reveals it to us, as in time-lapse photography.

Nicholas Evans-Cato painting.

Evans-Cato investigated the geometry of an explosion and returned to paint the tree again. He had adopted a different perspective. The whole cannot be formed or seen from any single point of view.

Tree and explosion.

AN EXAMPLE FROM MEDICINE

I asked my good friend Frank Wilson, who I introduced in chapter 4, about these elements of creativity, perceiving and conceiving, and whether they are familiar to him in his own creative practice. Frank is a neurologist, and he told me that sensibility is, indeed, connected to the art of diagnosis in medicine, which is a process of sensing (perception) and conceptualizing, and back again.

My question provoked in Frank "a flood of memories of being in the emergency room making decisions about people with sudden onset of serious illness. How did I manage to do the right thing? What did I 'smell' and why?" he wondered.

Frank continued: "I suppose medicine would always be an incredibly rich reservoir of stories with implications about how we perceive, or why we seem to select one aspect of a situation or a scene to dwell on, rather than another." He then proceeded to write me a detailed description of one incident.

I saw [this patient] when I was working in an emergency room. I like this story because two different observers with vastly different backgrounds and (officially) nonoverlapping responsibilities in their jobs made their way to the same conclusion about this patient almost as soon as [we] saw him.

The patient was a young man, obviously healthy and athletic, who came to our ER about three in the morning complaining of severe back pain. On this particular night, the place had pretty much emptied by about two in the morning, and I—the only doc on duty—had taken the opportunity to get horizontal on a couch in the doctor's lounge. So out of a sound sleep I heard the nurse knocking at the door, saying, "Doctor Wilson, you have a patient."

I rolled out and started my "wake-up, wake-up" routine while walking to the exam room. I went in, and the patient and I started talking; he told me he was a meter reader for the gas company, and that afternoon had stumbled and fallen down walking up to someone's house. At the time, he didn't think he'd injured himself and completed his shift. The pain woke him up out of sleep and was so bad it alarmed him, so he came in to be checked. I was still pretty sleepy but dutifully ran through the standard mechanical tests, having him change posture, move his legs, and so on, and checked his reflexes. Still drowsy, and for no particular reason, I got out my stethoscope and listened to his chest. On one side everything was fine; on the other side, I could hear no sounds at all, ... no movement of air in and out of the lung. That woke me up!

I rechecked to be sure I wasn't hallucinating and more or less bolted out of the room, where the nurse and the receptionist were just hanging around, waiting to see what I'd say. I told them the young man had a collapsed lung (pneumothorax) and I needed to talk to the surgeon on call (not in the hospital).

I don't know what sort of reaction I expected from these two women (they had been doing the night shift together for at least ten years), but the receptionist burst out laughing and slapped her friend on the back in a sort of high-five gesture.

"See? What'd I tell you?" she said.

I looked at her in disbelief. This woman was a lovely but crusty woman in her fifties who had never had any formal medical training, but had been immersed in the goings-on of the ER for a long time and obviously felt herself a part of the place. I turned to her and asked, "Dodi, you knew he had a pneumothorax? How?!!"

She grinned with a sort of feigned shyness and said, "The way he walked. They all walk that way."

For a long time after this experience I tried to figure out what had made me listen to this guy's lungs, and I never figured it out. Something made me do it.

The receptionist has no skin in this game of diagnosis—if she makes a mistake, she's the only one who knows. Not so for the doctor.

This happened early in my three-year ER career ... and it taught me a crucial lesson: everybody who works in the ER becomes attuned to everything they see and hear, as I suppose all the men working on a fishing boat are attuned to complex circumstances that are not directly their concern. As a result, I made it an official policy during my tenure [two years in charge] that I expected anyone observing a situation who felt something was being missed to speak up.

Near the end of my last year, a new ER doctor came to me and complained that a nurse had started an electrocardiogram on a new patient with chest pain without his having authorized her to do so. I remember looking him dead in the eye and saying, "Let me tell you something very simple. The nurses here know what they're doing. They will save your ass more times than you'll ever be able to count. My advice to you is to get off your high horse and kiss the ground they walk on."[4]

Frank's advice to the new ER doctor reminds me of something the late Gordon Peers (1909–1988) once wrote. He was a RISD professor and also Chief Critic of the school's European Honors Program.

Sensibility—by definition mental receptivity, ready discernment, as of truth—is probably one of the most important human traits available to the artist. Without this the artist becomes skilled, authoritative eclectic but not truly creative because it is the discernment of truth not previously discovered that proves the creativity of an action.[5]

THE OTHER WAY AROUND

Your conception can really mess with how you perceive something, especially if it precedes perception—as in a preconception. That is the message in the aphorism often attributed to French poet and philosopher Paul Valéry (1871–1945): "To see is to forget the name of the thing one sees." If you begin a portrait by drawing an "eye," "nose," and "mouth," you will draw what you know those features to be, and not be able to see the distinct and unique contours, shadowing, and continuity between where one feature ends and the contours, shadowing, and continuity of a cheek begins. Your knowledge of how these features look are limiting what you can see.

I could demonstrate that through a drawing exercise, but the best way I can convey the influence of a preconception on perception here is through a famous awareness test. Just watch this video of the "selective attention test" created by Daniel Simons and Christopher Chabris (http://www.youtube.com/watch?v=vJG698U2Mvo); if I tell you about it, the test will be ruined. Read on only after you've watched the video.

As the test's authors explain in their book about the subject:

Our minds don't work the way we think they do. We think we see ourselves and the world as they really are, but we're actually missing a whole lot.

[This illusion] reveals the numerous ways that our *intuitions* can deceive us, but it's more than a catalog of human failings. In the book, we also explain why people succumb to these everyday illusions and what we can do to inoculate ourselves against their effects. In short, we try to give you a sort of "x-ray vision" into your own minds, with the ultimate goal of helping you notice the invisible gorillas in your own life.[6]

I think this test illustrates the play between conception and perception, but I don't think intuition is the right word for it. You are asked to be selectively attentive to one aspect when taking the test. In this case, a preconception acts to select what you perceive. I think that if you were not asked to be selectively attentive to this aspect, you would in fact see the gorilla. The request made at the outset of this test corrupts your intuition.

THE ROOTS OF DISCOVERY AND INVENTION

Perceiving and conceiving can be understood as the root processes behind discovery and invention, which in effect is what creativity is. Really, really good observation—meaning perception unburdened by preconception and judgment—is how discoveries are made. As William James (1842–1910) wrote, "The great field for new discoveries is always the Unclassified Residuum. Round about the accredited and orderly facts of every science there ever flows a sort of dust-cloud of exceptional observations, of occurrences minute and irregular and seldom met with, which it always proves more easy to ignore than to attend to."[7] James, an American philosopher and psychologist, is considered by many to be one of the most influential thinkers of the nineteenth century.

Koestler offers Sherlock Holmes as an example of someone who observes intently but freely among different existing classifications.

> The genius of Sherlock Holmes manifested itself in shifting his attention to minute clues which poor Watson found too obvious to be relevant, and so easy to ignore. The psychiatrist obtains his clues from the casual remark, the seemingly irrelevant drift of associations; and he has learned to shift the emphasis from the patient's meaningful statements to his meaningless slips of the tongue, from his rational experiences to his irrational dreams.[8]

Discovery and invention are creative accomplishments in all fields, whether science and math oriented or the arts. There is a fine line between where discovery ends and invention begins. In the same way that the back-and-forth between perceiving and conceiving works in this chapter—as, for example, in drawing from life or giving a medical diagnosis—so too, and for the same reason, does the back-and-forth work between discovery and invention: one feeds and clarifies the other. Jacques Hadamard (1865–1963), a French mathematician who also wrote on creativity, presents the idea of a fine line between a discovery and invention in his example of the barometer and lightning rod.

> [Evangelista] Toricelli has observed that when one inverts a closed tube on the mercury trough, the mercury ascends to a certain determinate height: this is a discovery; but in doing this, he has invented the barometer; and there are plenty of examples of scientific results which are just as much discoveries as inventions. [Benjamin] Franklin's invention of the lightning rod is hardly different from his discovery of the electric nature of thunder.[9]

Thomas Edison inverted a discovery in his invention of the pho-
nograph. He had invented an apparatus that recorded the dots and
dashes of incoming Morse code as indentations on a rotating disc.
The disc was placed on a transmitting machine with a contact lever
that moved up and down according to those indentations. As the
contact lever traveled the dots and dashes, it produced an uninten-
tional rattling sound. If the disc rotated rapidly, the vibrating lever
hummed. Edison, who was hard of hearing, nevertheless noticed
this sound and conceived the reversal of his invention. By specifically creating indentations that came from sonic vibration, a lever
could then ride these indented grooves, and in this way replicate
the vibrations and the sounds that originally produced them. As
Koestler tells it,

> The rest was a matter of elaboration. Instead of a paper disc, Edi-
> son proposed to use a cylinder covered with soft tin-foil; instead of
> attaching the needle to a Morse-telegraph, he attached it to a mem-
> brane set into vibration by the waves of sound.... When it was fin-
> ished Edison shouted at it: "Mary had a little lamb." Then he turned
> the handle of the recording cylinder.
>
> The machine reproduced perfectly. Everybody was astonished....
> And that was that. To quote once more the jargon of communication
> engineering: the background "noise" of the vibrating lever had been
> turned into "information."[10]

INVESTING IN WHAT DOESN'T YET EXIST

Conceiving is an investment in what doesn't yet exist. It flows from
your perceptions, driven by your sensibility, to something abstract
that is waiting to become concrete. As you conceive, you are trying

to see ahead. A concept relates perceptions into a logical construct. It can form from an abstraction of something perceived.

Just as the storm gathers and regathers, never necessarily following a linear path, so too does the creative process fold and unfold. And so, to conceptualize, you return to gathering and tracking, finding fragments of patterns that will serve the ideas that can now become more concrete manifestations of the goal/ideal I wrote of in chapter 4. You oscillate around and towards those ideas, as when you were tracking, because you are tracking anew.

Conceptualizing, though, takes you beyond the goal/ideal, because it includes how the abstract relates to the realm of the concrete. It functions as a bridge. It takes your creative activity from the abstract into the practical making, toward the ideal. Attributes begin to emerge—attributes of what you will create. They give substance and density to the goal/ideal. In this context, density is a measure of quantity, as if your ideas are crystallizing.

The observer is often the artist's or designer's point of view, and it is important to recognize the role of the author's point of view in reaching a concept. The structure of a bee's eyes is a matrix of hundreds of single eyes called ommatidia, each with its own lens. This structure causes the bee to see the visual information from each of the ommatidia arranged in a matrix not unlike the hexagonal matrix of the hive. You could say that the bee is building what it knows not to be there but literally *how* it sees. The same could be said for artists and designers.

Paolo Uccello (1397–1475) was an Italian painter and mathematician particularly celebrated for his masterpiece *The Battle of San Romano*. The triptych painting's three separate panels each hang in different museums: the Uffici in Florence, Louvre in Paris, and National Gallery in London.

What many do not know about Uccello is the remarkable contribution he made as an inventor of perspective. His perspective is unlike that developed by two other artists/architects whose work on the subject is taught in art schools: his contemporary Filippo Brunelleschi (1377–1446), and Alberto di Giovanni Alberti (1525–1599). Rather than a spatial field convergent on one or two points, Uccello's perspective is based, in essence, on a vanishing point wherever the viewer looks. He doesn't place objects within a gridded architectural field that vanishes to these points; instead, he focuses on the perspectival construction of the floating objects themselves.

While the typical method of perspective lent itself to square and rectangular scenes and objects, Uccello's system could equally tackle free-form objects such as horses and people. Unlike the perspective systems of the time that were based on a convergent infinity, Uccello's perspective was based on a dynamic immensity. Wherever you look is the trajectory of perspective.

The Battle of San Romano by Paolo Uccello, National Gallery, London.

Uccello drew a sphere covered with pyramids that represents, in a way, his view of the world: a world that is immense and continues infinitely no matter which direction you look.

If you are being truly creative and something new is coming forth, an emergence within the concrete will trigger surprise and joy. In my experience, these are the emotions in creative practice that confirm your concept. You are ready to engage with the next element of the creative process.

Storm's-eye view 7.

SEEING AHEAD

In chapter 5 of *Through the Looking Glass* by Lewis Carroll (1832–1898), Alice and the White Queen have an exchange that ends with a comment by the White Queen that has always struck me.

"I don't understand you," said Alice. "It's dreadfully confusing!"

"That's the effect of living backwards," the Queen said kindly: "it always makes one a little giddy at first—"

"Living backwards!" Alice repeated in great astonishment. "I never heard of such a thing!"

"—but there's one great advantage in it, that one's memory works both ways."

"I'm sure *mine* only works one way," Alice remarked. "I can't remember things before they happen."

"It is a poor sort of memory that only works backwards," the Queen remarked.[1]

What kind of memory works forward? I asked myself. Insight? Intuition? Imagination? In describing creativity, all three of these faculties of the human mind tend to be used interchangeably. Nevertheless, each describes something that allows you to move ahead without necessarily knowing where you are going. They are ways of seeing into the future of creative work. As the great Russian composer Modest Mussorgsky (1839–1881) wrote in the dedication to his opera *Boris Godunov*, "The artist believes in the future because he lives in it."

Not only the artist is living in the future; so is anyone who creates. Something I wrote in the introduction bears repeating. We see ahead when we make designs that are materialized in the future, when we write problems that anticipate solutions, when we link one step to another in navigating our lives and the way through anything, especially the empty page, writer's block, confusion, chaos, needs, and questions. These are creative acts.

Let's look at these three terms—insight, intuition, and imagination—more closely and explore the role they play in creativity.

Insight is a deep understanding of the inner nature of things, the capacity to see the potential in things, to see where *this* goes. Insight = wonder + experience + recognition. With insight, you ask yourself, What could this be? I find that insight is something that can emerge through diagrams and outlines. Diagrams and outlines can launch a creative work as a notation of the insight. They do so by holding together everything that is known about the creative work to be undertaken and absorbing what is coming.

Intuition is a flash of knowing something without the conscious steps of reasoning. I believe it depends on insight and imagination.

Imagination is the forming of a mental "image" or virtual representation of something that is not present to the senses or has never before been wholly perceived in reality. It is an investment you make in what doesn't yet exist. It has sensory attributes that can be perceived internally, in much the same way as you perceive virtual realities when you dream. It is a mistake to see the role of the imagination as primarily fantastic. It requires a psychic commitment.

Imagination can transform a concept from the noumenal to phenomenal. In the introduction of *The Poetics of Space*, Bachelard proposed "the imagination as a major power of human nature.... [B]y the swiftness of its actions, the imagination separates us from the past as well as from reality: it faces the future." He writes, "The poem ... interweaves real and unreal," and "actual conditions are no longer determinant."[2]

The distinction between real and unreal doesn't exist in our dreams. For more than two years, I painted my dreams. My practice was to sketch what I could remember on waking, trying to remain true to the image of the dream, and returning later in the day to paint them. As lines were drawn, the memory could be "drawn out." This, I think, is because as the lines appeared on the page, they could actually be seen and no longer needed to be remembered. The drawing was a kind of repository for memory fragments as I remembered more.

Often, the process I am describing would present a dilemma. For example, let's say that I had been sitting at a table in the dream. I could see what was on and under the table. The awareness in the dream of both what is on and beneath the table were images in my mind's eye. They each had equal presence and visibility without seeming strange. And so I painted my dreams as *I* saw them;

things that were behind other things would be visible. Often, the sequence of images within one dream would jump around, so they could never be told with a single linear timeline. The images I created have aspects that are like X-rays and other aspects that are like a time lapse.

Watercolor of a dream.

I asked a friend, poet Stuart Blazer, about the play of real and unreal in his poetry. He told me he enjoys

the synchromesh transmission shifting between "unreal" & "real" within the line, the stanza, the whole thing. What was deemed "unreal" in a certain context can suddenly appear as an aspect of landscape in certain weather conditions. Some inwardly manufactured/received "vision" snowballs its way down an observable mountain, gathering disparate material as well as momentum. The confusion, the hinge, the between-place, "the taint" declares itself.[3]

Here is an excerpt from Stuart's poem "Landscape with Palms and Ocean":

Ideas vegetate,
take root
as dispersal, fog
a mental pollen
for human bees
busily making honey.

Idyllic landscapes
with ocean and palms
become one more paradise
deferred, adored idols
sacrificed to the actual.

What stays beautiful
is vision itself
as physical fact, more
than anything looked at.

Solid available light.

Silence that speaks its need.[4]

GLYPHS

A man came to our architectural firm asking us to design a restaurant in a particular space. He had some ideas. He talked about a French-Italian menu. He was calling the restaurant "33." He and his partner were both 33 years old. The street address was also 33.

In his memoir of the French artist and sculptor Henri Gaudier-Brzeska, the expatriate American poet and critic Ezra Pound (1885–1972)—a looming figure in early modernist literature—described poems as image texts, and images in verse as "a VORTEX, from which, and through which, and into which, ideas are constantly rushing."[5] That sounds much like a storm. I think this description also fits a glyph, which can serve as a kind of armature for the work that is to come. The man who had come to our firm, as he talked, drew the two 3s back-to-back on a napkin. It was a kind of glyph, and it set the design in motion.

We found an axis in the restaurant space. There was a specific mirrored geometry that hinged on the axis we located. The sign for the restaurant was literally passing through the exterior wall in a mirrored and three-dimensional way so that it was legible from both the inside and outside. All the design elements came from the folded-mirrored geometry in the doodle of the two back-to-back 3s.

Hieroglyphs are a combination of phonetic text and pictograms. For instance, the word for cat is a combination of three characters that are phonetic, mi + i + w, derived from the cat's "miaow," and one picture sign of a cat. We make glyphs when we doodle. The drawing Woodland made when he drew his fingers through the sand is a kind of glyph. Glyphs, pictograms, and phonetic text give image or sound for eye and ear and body to resonate in.

The dictionary defines matrix as "that within which or within and from which something originates, takes form, or develops." Some of the words in that definition are remarkably similar to Pound's vortex. To me, glyphs often appear like dense matrices seen from a distance. I think they are the anatomy of an idea.

INSIGHT PLANS

Architects make small diagrams, thumbnail sketches, in figuring out a project. These diagrams are a form of glyphs. We draw them constantly, in sketchbooks, and on envelopes and napkins. A thumbnail sketch defines a project's architectural anatomy. It is a matrix, with all the contingencies of the situated project acting, seen from the vantage point of the conceptual whole. What is a glyph for a writer is a thumbnail sketch to the architect. I like to call these, based on the recommendation of my friend Blazer, "insight plans." They need to be done constantly, like the recitation of a mantra. They are a dense matrix seen from a distance: the anatomy of an idea.

In the drawing and redrawing of insight plans, the gesture of its lines becomes familiar, and at the same time, because of its nakedness, the drawing is scrutinized. These are naked drawings, stripped of any excessive mark or expression. Each time one is drawn, each starting point, length, or trajectory of each mark is scrutinized. How one mark meets, intersects, or sits relative to another is questioned. The hand is the pioneer of the page, a course gone over and over again, the same meridians, the same intersections, branches, and boundaries done repeatedly, as if to remember something that is in the making; it is a memory in process, or inverse memory. A view from a tower is constructed by these gestures, and anatomy is recognizable. Insight plans are armatures for design.

Insight plans figured when we were commissioned as architects to design an addition to an existing prefabricated church that had been built in the 1970s. The addition was to be a children's chapel. Before doing any design, we spoke with parishioners and the pastors, in interviews and informal conversations, to learn about their needs and aspirations for the church. They stated that they had outgrown their existing building and needed more space "to breathe." That language choice held an intuition for the project.

The chapel's shape, as a semiattached pavilion extension of the existing education wing, was set by a master plan. The footprint was to be a trapezoid. A more open space on the exterior of the west side of the chapel was created by swinging the chapel's west wall in so that it was not parallel to its east wall, forming the trapezoid.

The existing church had a steeple with a spire that you can purchase from a catalog. The steeple had been placed on the building by a crane.

My partners and I, in one of our presentations to the church members, were embarrassed to realize that we had forgotten the steeple on our physical model of the existing church. When we added it, the spire kept getting knocked off. I began to wonder, "What is a spire, anyway?" So I looked up the word spire in the dictionary. What I found addressed the purpose, history, aspirations of openness, and desire for expansion the church members had as well as the specific diagram of the chapel. The "accident" of neglecting the steeple led to attention to "spire," which gave us an insight into what the design should be.

As you know by now, having made it here to chapter 7, finding the origins of words, the etymology, and how and why words have come to have their meanings when we use them, is important to me in understanding creativity. The English word spire comes from the Latin word *spirare*, which means "to breathe." It shares its root with *spirit* as well as with *spiral*—a form that expands and contracts like breath. *Respire* and *expire* are related words, as is *inspiration*.

At the same time, we were trying to figure out the diagram of this chapel, with its trapezoidal footprint and corresponding walls. The question was how to resolve the structure from opposite walls that are not parallel. We came up with complicated structural solutions aimed at resolving the different angles of the walls. Running through the possible solutions for a specific problem is a process of envisioning what could be. It is a process of imagination.

Suddenly, I had a thought to keep the structural order that framed each of these walls so that they remain square or "true" to themselves. What I found was that the structural order would continue up one wall, across the roof and back down the opposite wall, across the floor, and back up the first wall. The order does not form a closed frame but instead spirals around, like a string wrapping the space of the chapel. The spiral tightens at the narrow end of the chapel and expands toward the opposite end. This would make the entire pavilion a sort of spire.

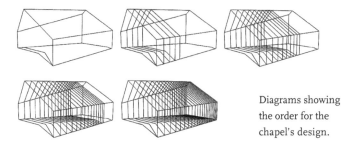

Diagrams showing the order for the chapel's design.

This became a convincing diagram for the design of the chapel: the geometry of the ceiling/roof and floor spirals north, setting the structure, windows, and ceiling/wall acoustic fins.

When we presented the idea to the church, we made another discovery of how the idea related to the two historic churches from which two parishes had come together to comprise the current congregation at the church. The church on the left in the illustration has its structure poking out from under the skin of its siding, and its roof is sucked in. The one on the right has its structure out of sight, within its skin of siding. It is as though the two churches where inhaling and exhaling: the body carving a cavity, the skin taut, revealing structure on the inhale, and the body and skin relaxing on the exhale.

Front facade of historic churches.

Truly, the diagram we presented met the criterion I had heard: space to breathe.

View inside the finished chapel.

A LESSON FROM KLEE

Early on in my career as a teacher, I had a unique opportunity to witness the workings of insight, intuition, and imagination. I had given a class of students a full-scale image of Klee's watercolor painting *Polyphonically Framed White*, and asked them to build the third dimension using only white museum board and white glue.

Unlike cardboard or illustration board, museum board has a consistent material all the way through. That means a white museum board is white all the way through. One of my students who is now a practicing architect based in Connecticut, John R. Schroeder, decided that he was going to build the third dimension of the plaid-like grid of Klee's painting by assigning each color in the painting a different dimension in depth and build each rectangle of color as hollow rectangular tubes of differing depths. So starting with a single piece of rectangular white museum board as his base, the different-length tubes arranged in the organization of the painting, John intended to form a growing depth, with the center rectangle, the white rectangle of Klee's painting, the deepest.

I spoke with John before he began to build. I wanted to understand why he was doing this and the source of his approach. He couldn't say beyond that he had had a kind of insight about a relationship of color and depth he wanted to realize. Something about his sense of purpose made me step aside and just watch.

John worked through the night, building the arranged cluster of hollow white museum board tubes. When he had finished, he held his project up to the indirect sunlight coming through the north side of the building. The white tubes of differing lengths refracted the light and re-created the colors of Klee's painting.

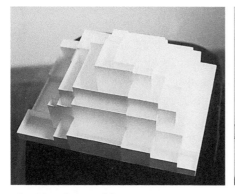

John Schroeder's model.

Klee's painting and an untouched scan of a Kodachrome slide taken of John's model can be found in the insert to this book. The image of John's model is a view from the bottom of the model held up and exposed to indirect northern sunlight.

I think John intuited the relationship of color to depth. Different colors have different focal lengths. Perhaps in his attentiveness to Klee's painting, John *felt* the different depths of color. His intuition formed the impulse to build the varying heights of tubes out of white museum board. The tubes reflected light so that the object when viewed with indirect light took on a range of colors from a cool to warm spectrum.

What John made also made me wonder whether Klee might have seen an object like that which John built and then painted *it*. It is possible; after all; Klee was a teacher at the Bauhaus, where many form studies were made out of white board.[6]

REITERATIVE CYCLES

The examples of the chapel and John's creation again raise the notion of reiteration that I wrote about in chapter 1. Reiteration is common to a storm and creativity. The creative process is cyclic, going through reiterative cycles that anticipate what is to come. It is not uncommon that the creative process brings about discoveries of something that was already in existence but not yet recognized, just as the scientific community didn't recognize Wegener's discovery of continental drift (discussed in chapter 3) for four decades.

The chapel's diagram anticipated a good solution, but also revealed something about the church's history. John's strategy for building the three-dimensional interpretation of Klee's painting anticipated the phenomenon of light refracting the colors of the painting, but also points to a possible history of what Klee himself was observing when he originally made the painting.

Over the span of a creative practice, something else is revealed about our calling or vocation. I am referring to the personal narrative we each form. I mentioned this in chapter 1. The lives we live end up being the qualifications for the vocation we take up. In other words, had Woodland not been a Boy Scout who studied Morse code, the lines he saw when he drew his fingers through the sand would have meant nothing to him. Uncanny insights like these allow us see into the future but depend on the past—more specifically, our own pasts. That is how I understand the White Queen's reference to backward memory as being the inverse of imagination.

MORE ON IMAGINING AND IMAGINATION

Imagination is an instrument for seeing. It takes you on a ramble through choices and leads you to concrete attributes, from percept (the object of perception) to concept and then to something realized that you can perceive again. As I wrote earlier, it is an investment you make in what doesn't yet exist.

When you have a concept that is abstract and need to push things to the next step in creative practice, you can use your imagination. In essence, you freeze the conceptual process and ask yourself questions. There are general questions: What could this be? What is possible? What are my options? As you answer, you are investing in the future. And there are more specific questions. If you are a designer, you might ask, What if I use this material, or that material? If you are writing a novel, you might ask, What if I make the mail carrier a woman instead of a man, and give her a limp? If you are a scientist, working at the bench in a lab, you might ask, What if I introduce this into the petri dish?

This is how you use your imagination to "see" possible outcomes before they are ripe and ready, to get a sense of where you might go from abstract to concrete.

Imagination takes you away from the perspective of the here and now of which I wrote in chapter 2. In creative practice, when you reach the point of imagination you have long since made your problem, and your attentiveness to the here and now has shifted to something forward looking. It also broadens your perspective, because while your individual observations are key to the creative process, as you reach the point when you will make something you have to see it as a whole, and that cannot be done from any single perspective.

Imagining has an effect on what you think. As an activity, imagination generates or evokes novel situations, ideas, or other individual instances of subjective, conscious experiences in your mind—something philosophers call qualia, from the Latin *qualis*, meaning "what kind" or "what sort." Imagining, by its very nature, is not a direct or passive experience but rather a subjective activity.

Psychologists use the term imagination to describe a process humans go through to revive percepts of objects in their minds they had perceived with their senses. They sometimes call it "imaging" or "imagery," and what you imagine is, as is said, seen in your "mind's eye."

Imagination has all sorts of practical functions, which is part of why it is so important at this stage of the creative process, when you are making the abstract concrete. It allows you to "see" something from the perspective of someone else. It allows you to project possible futures. It is the mind's function that you use to change how something you've perceived will be realized in the concrete. You make decisions based on your imagination, because you respond to your imaginings.

Insight, intuition, and imagination come from an intense focus on what is happening in the present, with the work right there in front of you, but give views to what is to come and what has been. As Eliot wrote:

Time present and time past
Are both perhaps present in time future
And time future contained in time past.
If all time is eternally present
All time is unredeemable.[7]

Storm's-eye view 8.

CONNECTING

Plankton comes from the Greek word for "wanderer" or "drifter," and refers to any organism that floats and moves by way of the currents in the water, as opposed to having the ability to move itself. Recently, scientists discovered that phytoplankton—the tiny, microscopic, single-cell organisms floating in the top layer of the ocean—may serve themselves by affecting weather and climate. Phytoplankton are sensitive to ultraviolet radiation; when sun exposure is high, they produce a metabolite that makes their cell walls less vulnerable to ultraviolet rays. Bacteria in the ocean water then break down this metabolite, which is converted and filtered into the air. There, it forms dustlike particulates of the perfect size on which water molecules can condense. When that happens, it makes clouds, increasing the cloud cover that protects the vulnerable phytoplankton from ultraviolet radiation. The entire cycle takes only a few days.

This is just one of countless examples of how everything is connected, somehow, from the astronomical to the metabolic. We may not always see these connections. For me, creativity is making connections or making the existing connections visible. As discussed in chapter 7, insight, intuition, and imagination involve seeing from other perspectives, projecting possible futures, and combining multiple views simultaneously in the mind's eye. Patterns and linkages are recognizable when a "vision" is empowered by insight, intuition, and imagination. Previously unseen connective threads lead the way toward transformative observations and thinking. Recognizing the threads of connection is inextricable from creative thought.

Steve Jobs (1955–2011), an American entrepreneur and inventor, cofounded Apple, Inc., and guided the company through a veritable transformation of the personal computer and consumer electronics fields. Apple has become synonymous with outstanding creativity and design. In a 1996 interview, Jobs was asked why more products aren't made with the aesthetics of great design. Part of his answer was a description of how he saw creativity.

> Creativity is just connecting things. When you ask creative people how they did something, they feel a little guilty because they didn't really do it, they just saw something. It seemed obvious to them after a while. That's because they were able to connect experiences they've had and synthesize new things. And the reason they were able to do that was that they've had more experiences or they have thought more about their experiences than other people.
>
> Unfortunately, that's too rare a commodity. A lot of people in our industry haven't had very diverse experiences. So they don't have enough dots to connect, and they end up with very linear solutions without a broad perspective on the problem. The broader one's

understanding of the human experience, the better design we will have.[1]

The definition Jobs gives is straightforward. Creativity is connecting; it is something creative people see, not necessarily always something they do; creators draw connections from their experiences.

DARWIN AS A CONNECTOR

Darwin is one of the most creative connectors of all time. He changed the way we understand life. His theory of natural selection explains the main process causing the modification and origin of species. Natural selection explains how evolution happens.

The elegance and simplicity of natural selection is astonishing. The theory comprises three observations that Darwin elevated to principles: organisms produce more offspring than will survive; traits vary within a species; and these traits or variations are carried from one generation to the next. The theory of natural selection is the seemingly obvious consequence of connecting these three observations. Traits of an organism that survive through generations define the species and variations or mutations that are carried forward to bring about the origin of a new species. An understanding of the many permutations through the many generations is necessary to make this comprehensible.

Darwin certainly fits Jobs's description of creative people as those "able to connect experiences they've had and synthesize new things," and able to do so because "they've had more experiences or they have thought more about their experiences than other people." As discussed in chapter 2, Darwin boarded the HMS *Beagle* at age twenty-two for his five-year trip around the globe as a naturalist-guest of Captain Fitzroy—an extraordinary experience certainly not available to the average person. He was a budding naturalist when he got the invite. Fitzroy was looking to both equip the voyage for scientific exploration and for someone who could serve as a companion on the long journey. Darwin was seasick for a big part of his time onboard, but he kept active collecting and sending home the specimens of life he discovered on land. He wrote letters and kept a detailed journal.

Immediately after the voyage, Darwin spelled out the three principles of natural selection in his notes. His recognition of the three principles required no augmentation; no special equipment or instrument was necessary to observe that any of the three principles were true. What was revolutionary was that Darwin connected them, and in so doing, radically shifted our outlook on just about everything.

Although Darwin came to his theory in his twenties, it wasn't until he was fifty years old that he published it in his book *On the Origin of Species*.[2] The common misconception is that he delayed publication for decades because he feared the impact the concept of evolution would have on the world. As Stephen Jay Gould argues in his essay "Can We Complete Darwin's Revolution?" the concept of evolution was one of the most widespread unorthodox ideas being pursued by scientists during Darwin's time.[3] What was unique, according to Gould, was Darwin's explanation of the mechanism of evolution through his theory of natural selection. And once understood correctly, his theory would change the way life and its meaning were understood.

Connecting the three principles of overpopulation, variation, and inheritance of variation, Darwin concluded that species evolve and originate by many generations producing permutations of inherited traits. No overarching purpose to this lengthy process is necessary other than the accumulation of what each generation may choose through reproduction and the consequences of those choices. Not only is purpose across time unnecessary, progress of the evolved species across time is irrelevant as well. As Gould points out, that is why Darwin initially refused to use the word evolution: it implied a progressive change.

Darwin's idea was radical: species vary and originate based on individuals' reproductive choices as well as chance encounters with the adaptive success of the traits that are passed through the generations. This was difficult to recognize and hard to accept because it meant the human species was no longer the pinnacle or destiny of millions of years of "progressive" evolution. Instead, our species results from the survival of chance variations carried down through millions of years of successive generations, just like any other species alive today.

In making a connection between the three principles that are core to natural selection, Darwin also saw an analogous connection between naturalism and the economic theory of Adam Smith.[4] Smith's laissez-faire economics (from the French, literally meaning "let [them] do," but colloquially meaning "let it be" or "leave it alone") was based on the idea that a well-functioning economy could emerge through the collective role of individuals' struggle for personal profit. Darwin studied Smith, and saw the connections between laissez-faire capitalism and the ecosystem that results from many individual organisms seeking reproductive success without purpose imposed from above.

Darwin saw the connections between his observations regarding overpopulation, variation, and inheritance of variation precisely because he was freed of the preconception of evolution or preconception of species' development having an overarching purpose. He could see the connection because he was able to question the preconception of evolution as a progressive path with humans as the penultimate destination. He was able to recognize the *material* explanation because he could question a supernatural spiritual explanation. Darwin was well aware of the radicalism of his ideas and biases in place that blinded others to his understanding. As he wrote in his notebook in October 1838, "Love of the deity, effect of organization, oh you materialist! ... Why is thought being a secretion of brain, more wonderful than gravity a property of matter? It is our arrogance, our admiration of ourselves."[5]

Darwin was aware of the radical shift his theory would produce if understood. Just as Copernicus's theories had displaced the earth out of the center of the universe, Darwin took us off the predestined pedestal of life-forms. Darwin identified the mechanism of species development by making connections of facts out in the open for others to see and make, if they had not been blinded by the comfortable assumptions of the times.

CONNECTING ACROSS SILOS

Jobs demonstrated his definition of creativity as "connecting things" as well as disciplines and people when building the Macintosh some thirty years ago. He wanted to revolutionize the computer industry by making computers intuitive to use and more widely available. So he established a team of individuals from varied disciplines that included a brilliant self-educated dropout, an artist, a doctoral candidate in medicine and philosophy, a musician, and an archeologist, and brought them together with computer scientists to show how the values of the arts could be integrated with computer technology and engineering.

Guy Tribble was the manager of software development and a member of that original Macintosh design team. It was a time when computers were much slower than today and, as he explained, "any extra computing cycles you had should be used to make the spread sheet run faster." The Macintosh team's approach was different. As Tribble recalled, "We said, well with this very precious computer power let's devote some of it to painting pictures on the screen"— and in doing so, the Mac became a computer that could be used intuitively.[6]

Bringing together several disciplines broadens and challenges each discipline's thinking. Jobs did this through the varied expertise each member brought to a design team. Negotiation of the different practices of several disciplines can shake preconceptions, and things that were previously unseen are then out in the open for a discovery to be made. In a similar way, merging two previously independent fields can revolutionize entire fields—as happened in astronomy.

Up until Johannes Kepler (1571–1630), astronomy was a branch of mathematics and understood through geometry. The purity of geometry is what drew Kepler to astronomy. The German astronomer began his study convinced that the motion of planetary bodies was perfect and circular. But he started thinking of planetary orbits as a physical problem, as bodies being swept through space and affecting each other. That led Kepler to an understanding that some point within the arcs of the orbits must be the source of a force that played a role in the planets' revolution. This source, of course, is the gravitational pull of the sun.

It was Kepler's introduction of physical forces into astronomy (what he called "celestial physics" and has since become the field of astrophysics) that allowed him to describe the actual motion of planets around the sun. Just as Darwin later, he developed three laws, in this case about planetary motion: the orbit of a planet is an ellipse with the sun at one of the two foci; a line segment joining a planet and the sun sweeps out equal areas during equal intervals of time; and the square of the orbital period of a planet is proportional to the cube of the semi-major axis of its orbit. The first law describes the geometric path of planetary motion; the second law describes the changing speed of planetary motion at any given point along an orbit; and the third law compares the period and radius of orbit of different planets. What had previously been blinding—Kepler's obsession with circular orbits—gave way when Kepler sought the connections between physics and astronomy. That canceled out his preconceptions and made his discovery possible.

CONSTRUCTED CONNECTIONS

The connections of how something is constructed or put together are as important as the conceptual connections of the above examples. As discussed in chapter 5, tectonics, the relation between things, is a language for architects, and is expressed through the design of details and junctures between one element and another, or one space and another. The physical sticking together of the architecture is how meaning is expressed. Cohesion refers to the physical aspect of connecting. The word comes to us from the Latin *cohaere*, meaning "stick or stay together." In a storm, cohesion holds together all the material the storm has gathered. All the conditions of the storm exist prior to the storm, but it is the compounding of the conditions that produces the storm. How the conditions are compounded, how they interrelate and transform each other, causes the storm to build, propel, and become a distinct cohesive entity. In creative practice, cohesion is what does the holding. Cohesion may be of words, facts, materials, sounds, movement, or space. It may be process or product. It may be combinations of many, or all these.

But cohesion describes only the holding or sticking together of quantity, like the density or crystallization of ideas I mentioned in chapter 6. Linguistically, words that are connected by "and," "but," or grammatical links are cohesively held together. Words that are connected become coherent through a context of meaning. In creative practice, the transformation from quantity to quality requires coherence. Coherence holds the quantity together with meaning. How it is held together communicates that meaning.

Coherence can come from connections made through direct and observable relations of cause and effect, interdependencies, or a loose associative logic. These connections can be made by recognizing patterns or literally with the material of the creative work. In a process generally filled with uncertainty and doubt, meaningful connections are handholds for moving ahead. Like the rope of a rope bridge you hold to get across a gulf, the connective threads are held onto, guiding you from one step of the process to another. In filmmaking, as in architecture, what structurally holds it together is what also does the expressing.

The filmic structure of Stanley Kubrick's *The Shining* is built from the cinematography that gets progressively more and more compressed. The film opens with a bird's-eye pan shot from a helicopter over a vast landscape, continues with the wide-angle shot of the Overlook Hotel, and then wide-angle shots of large empty gathering spaces and lounges. Through the shots and transitions, Kubrick structurally communicates agoraphobia. As the film progresses, the shots narrow into repeated one-point perspectival views: from the point of view of the boy on the Big Wheel riding through the hotel's endless hallways, to the claustrophobic reflections of the stainless steel cabinets in the kitchen, to the culmination in the most compressed, monochromatic view within the hedge labyrinth in a blizzard.

ANALOGIES: CONNECTIONS FOUND THROUGH ASSOCIATIVE LOGIC

Our human brain size, with its large associative cortexes, makes us conducive to so-called crossings that are the basis of associative logic. Most other mammals have a brain structured like a "bucket brigade"—a path of exchange along a singular line.[7] Something triggers the mammal's brain and there is a response. The relationship of the trigger and response is repeated and reinforced over its lifetime, making it less likely than the human brain to have these crossings of associations we have when making analogies and seeing the connections between things previously thought to be disconnected.

The connections creative people recognize have many forms: visual similarities, patterns, and similar analogical structures or relations. Koestler cites many examples of analogies drawn in the mind of scientists and inventors at the moment they made their breakthrough discoveries. One was Élie Metchnikoff (1845–1916).

A Russian biologist, zoologist, and protozoologist, Metchnikoff did pioneering research into the immune system and is credited with discovering macrophages—a type of white blood cell critical to the body's defenses against diseases such as cancer. Metchnikoff shared the 1908 Nobel Prize in Medicine for his work on phagocytosis, the name for the process in which macrophages engage.

Koestler describes how Metchnikoff, alone with his microscope,

> was observing the life of the mobile cells in the transparent larvae of starfish, and idly threw a few rose-thorns among them. The thorns were promptly surrounded by the larvae and dissolved inside their transparent bodies—they had been gobbled up and digested. This reminded him of what happens when a human finger is infected by a splinter: it will be surrounded by pus which, like the starfish larvae, will attack and try to digest the intruder.[8]

The analogy allowed him to "see" possible outcomes before they were ripe and ready, to get a sense that allowed him to go from the abstract to concrete. Mechnikoff drew a connection between the rose thorn and a splinter, and between the reaction, and discovered the role of antibodies.

Johannes Gutenberg (ca. 1398–1468) provides another example of associative logic, or analogy, from Koestler. Gutenberg invented his press for printing with movable type, as opposed to the engraved blocks, which when rubbed, transferred an impression to paper, that were used at the time, by applying associations made between machine practices from other trades to printing. Specifically, he analogized to coin punching and the cast seal, which led to the idea of typecasting. Punched coins had relief, and the cast seals were used in combinations (not a singular block or engraving, but rather an assembly of individually cast messages). They birthed an idea in Gutenberg's head: separate cast type assembled to make a page.

Gutenberg's associative logic, his connections, did not stop there. Rubbing the many cast letters that would form a page did not make precise prints. Koestler quotes Gutenberg's description of a critical observation he made when he took part in a wine harvest:

> I watched the wine flowing, and going back from the effect to the cause, I studied the power of this press which nothing can resist.... A simple substitution which is a ray of light.... To work then! God has revealed to me the secret that I demanded of Him.... I have had a large quantity of lead brought to my house and that is the pen with which I shall write.[9]

Thus, through the association of cast seals to lead cast type and wine press to paper printing press, Gutenberg invented the movable typeface press.

Koestler also offers the example of Benjamin Franklin, who observed that a finger or pointed object, when brought close to an electrified body, would draw a stronger spark than a blunt object. Franklin then drew an analogy between a cloud and electrified body, concluding that lightning was an electric discharge phenomenon. He also realized that if pointed objects were placed on houses and ships, they could draw the electricity out of a cloud, directing it through an attached wire down to the ground (for the house) or to the water (for the ship), and thus offering security from an electric fire. Thus was invented the lightning rod.

Franklin needed a rod high enough to point to the cloud, but encountered difficulties. The solution came during a daydream, sparked by a deep memory: his boyhood experience of floating on a lake for hours, drifting across the lake, attached to a kite. The kite was an elegantly simple solution for discharging a cloud with a point.[10]

CONNECTING DRIVEN BY CALLING

In his book *The Soul's Code*, psychologist and scholar James Hillman (1926–2011) wrote about what he called "the acorn," "daimon," or soul that proclaims itself in a defining image/moment of a young person's life.[11] He saw this as a third definer of character and calling, along with nature and nurture. Hillman described the assertion of the daimon as a "disturbance" in the existing nurture/nature model. Often what is considered as symptoms of an illness or bad behavior, according to Hillman, are expressions of the daimon fighting for the individual's existence—an intuitive act of distinguishing, forming, and following one's individuality. These intuitions contrast with "tuition" or learning, and therefore are often noncompliant with norms and conventions in schools.

The "calling" of the daimon or defining moment/image is kept alive internally by surviving the pressure of external narratives of nurture/nature determinism or the other influences. Like the dust devil that can trigger a storm, the will of the individual's self to exist triggers and gathers from the environment in turn, shaping it from a configuration of genes and circumstance of environment. Greatness is one of these expressions, forming into a whirlwind and reshaping the environment much like a little disturbance forming into a storm (and not petering out).

Our stories are a strong influence on how we gather experiences and make connections. This is one of the ways in which our own creativity, and what we choose to do with our lives, is mutually shaped.

Elliot Washor is an inspiring example of this. A creative educator, he applies Jobs's idea of creative connection in his work—work as an adult that is a creative reflection of his own experience as a boy.

Washor cofounded and codirects Big Picture Learning, an innovative approach to education that serves predominantly students for whom schools have failed. Big Picture Learning has established more than sixty schools nationwide structured around each student's self-assessment rather than standardized curriculum and rubrics. As Washor says, "We start with their personal stories, learn about their interests, and our students create and achieve in unusual ways."[12] Individual mentors and advisers support the student, crafting next steps and projects, providing reading materials, and setting up internships and workshops around the student's interests. The relationship of the adviser/mentor to the student is valued, as is finding the right people alongside whom the student can develop.

When I asked Washor where his sense of purpose comes from and what is the source of the creative spark behind Big Picture Learning, he gave answers about connections. He told me about his own personal experience of getting a better education outside school, from the people he knew: his father's best friend, who he knew as "Uncle Gab," and Uncle Gab's brother Harold, a man with infantile tuberculosis who had been "deformed" as a child when doctors removed part of his spine.

"He was a bright guy," Washor said. "He actually got a college degree. They put him in these schools for people they didn't want to look at, ... people they would call 'retarded.' And he fought that. And he was quite eccentric."

Washor told me about Harold's one-room apartment with "maybe between five and ten thousand books ... piled high up to the ceiling, three rows thick. Five-and-dime pocketbooks, but also the classics. So anytime I needed a book, I went and saw Harold."

This experience of connections and the empathy with people for whom schools had failed created the adult Washor, and influenced the creation of Big Picture Learning. "That part of me got connected to people who I have a lot of empathy for."

Washor created with those connections. An open system (storm or creative process) that feeds on energies and materials found in the environment is all the time building up more complex patterns of information (perceptions, memories, and ideas). It is active as well as reactive in its broader context.

SYNCHRONICITY: MEANINGFUL CONNECTIONS NOT (YET) UNDERSTOOD

In the creative process, you are constantly rethinking and rewriting the narrative of cause and effect, conversing with the characters, ever watchful of developments. Connections carry you through the process. They serve as confirmations of where you are or what you are doing, of the choices you have made. The connections could be the result of causal links, an intuitive leap of a chain of cause and effect. But they also could lack the causal explanation and be linked through meaning.

A chain of meaningful connections in a process that has starts and stops of activities, other processes, and scales can be powerful. Swiss psychologist Carl Gustav Jung (1875–1961) coined a term for it in the 1920s: *synchronicity*—the experience of two or more events that are not related causally or likely to occur together by chance, but when experienced do so in a way that their occurring together has meaning.

Notably, the concept of synchronicity is in no way intended to suggest that causality doesn't exist. Jung simply maintained that some events may be grouped by cause, but they may also be grouped by meaning.

Jung used the term *intellectual intuition* to describe what happens in your mind when synchronicity occurs. Might it explain, at least in part, what the White Queen meant when she told Alice, "It is a poor sort of memory that only works backwards"?[13] It turns out that this particular line from Carroll was one of Jung's favorite quotes.

Synchronicity is a concurrent event of powerful and meaningful connection. And what sort of memory works forward? Jung explained,

> only the ingrained belief in the sovereign power of causality that creates intellectual difficulties and makes it appear unthinkable that causeless events exist or could ever exist. But if they do, then we must regard them as creative acts, as the continuous creation of a pattern that exists from all eternity, repeats itself sporadically, and is not derivable from any known antecedents.[14]

"Coincidence," wrote the German philosopher Arthur Schopenhauer (1788–1860), "is the simultaneous occurrence of causally unconnected events." He observed that

> if we visualize each causal chain progressing in time as a meridian on the globe, then we may represent simultaneous events by the parallel circles of latitude.... All the events in a man's life would accordingly stand in two fundamentally different kinds of connection: firstly, in the objective, causal connection of the natural process; secondly, in a subjective connection which exists only in relation to the individual

who experiences it, and which is thus as subjective as his own dreams, whose unfolding content is necessarily determined, but in the manner in which the scenes in a play are determined by the poet's plot. That both kinds of connection exist simultaneously, and the self-same event, although a link in two totally different chains, nevertheless falls into place in both.... Thus everything is interrelated and mutually attuned.[15]

It seems to me that the connections one makes in the creative process can fall along arcs similar to Schopenhauer's meridians. The connections can fall a few degrees further along an existing arc of logic within an existing paradigm or problem within a discipline. Or they can emerge along another arc of logic different from the one you may have been following, as a few degrees further along an arc of logic from another discipline that happens to intersect the first arc of logic.

This is what Koestler refers to in his theory of "bisociative logic," which he believed is at work with all creativity. (Koestler saw it as two lines on their own planes, intersecting.) Bisociative logic is ideation that results from perceiving the intersection of two separate logics. The event of the intersection is no longer linked to one associative context but instead bisociated with two.

Koestler uses the example above of how Kepler brought questions of physical forces and movement to the predominantly geometric study of astronomy and thus produced a new paradigm of thinking. I propose an additional line to Koestler's model of bisociative logic that is subjective to the author and plays a critical role in creative discovery. It is not unlike the experience of synchronicity. When the arc of your own life intersects with an arc of the creative work in which you are engaged, it establishes a (from your own subjective view) noncausally related occurrence that leaps your work forward into a new realm.

The geometry of the model I propose is like Schopenhauer's meridians and Koestler's intersecting planes, but even more like the intersections of multiple arcs in the journey of water droplets in a storm. The droplets each have their own causal path and journey, rising and falling, condensing with other droplets, subjected to pressure and temperature, and then being drawn into the powerful cyclonic action, carrying the many causal arcs into an helical engine of connection and collision that moves determinedly on its way.

Water droplets' trajectory as the geometry of synchronicity.

Model done by John Schroeder. Photo scans from Kodachrome slides taken by author.

Paul Klee, *White Framed Polyphonically (Polyphon Gefasstes Weiss)*, 1930. Pen and watercolor on paper on cardboard. 33.3 × 24.5 cm. Zentrum Paul Klee, Bern.

Model seen frontally from below (frontal view of base of John Schroeder's model). Photographed using Kodachrome slide film, which is known to intensify the saturation of color, especially colors that fall within the warm end of the spectrum.

The subjective arc plays no small role. The experience of realizing the integration of separate trajectories is much like the experience of synchronicity.

When Woodward drew his fingers through the sand, it set off the "Eureka!" alert that led to his invention of the bar code, but only because he had learned Morse code as a Boy Scout. He recognized the logic of a code in the lines his fingers drew. Like Woodward's, the meaningful occurrence that takes your attention strikes you personally and hence you notice something not noticed by others—and a creative discovery is made. It feels the same way as the uncanny feeling one has when experiencing synchronicity. I think that is so because they are basically the same.

Synchronicity can be the experience of an event that appears in our sensory landscape that was previously "foreseen" by the unconscious, and hence the sense of confirmation of an intuition or insight: connections made between thoughts/sensations in the unconscious that precede and are confirmed by observations/discoveries made in sensory realm. It only becomes part of the conscious realm because the connection in the conscious mind called it into play. Two arcs of processes intersect again: the arc of processes in the unconscious that come from sensory input we may not even notice or have forgotten, and an arc of conscious thought processes. The "logic" of the synchronicity event may be invisible or unknowable by the conscious mind.

The possibility that John Schroeder "channeled" an object on which Klee based a painting (see chapter 7) is remarkable because neither John nor I nor the several Bauhaus scholars I spoke with have any knowledge that a similar object existed that Klee saw and painted. Workings outside our awareness produced that incredible insight. In other words, the insight came out of John's subjective unconscious.

You have a feeling of the uncanny, a surprise, an expansive sense of wonder, much like you feel at a collision of different arcs of thinking when coming up with an idea. It is a sense of expansion because your point of view has expanded to the multiple avenues.

We are all stricken with the tendency to reject previously unrecognized connections. They are illogical, they don't make sense, they don't fit. The matrices of thought can be woven tightly over time in our conscious minds, thereby making connections that don't fit the existing matrices seem mistaken.

We usually need to relinquish our grip on the intention of a project, the desire to know something we don't yet know, and the will to succeed in our creative endeavor—at least for enough time to pause or take a break, to allow the rich resource of the unconscious to offer up the unexpected connections made there. That is the topic of the next chapter: the role of pausing.

Storm's-eye view 9.

PAUSING

There is also an element of creativity, a "stage" in the process at which one should check out and take a pause. A storm does the same. It passes, dissipates, and scatters at different scales that are related to the different scales of the storm cell. A storm, when it stops over the ocean, gathers water and power, and unleashes them as it moves on again; so too, similarly, in the creative process.

This act of pausing may take many forms and be thought of in many ways. It is incubation. Fermentation. Mind wandering. Distraction. Giving up, only to start again. It is a retreat into unconsciousness. It is a kind of detachment from the process at hand.

Hadamard embraced the incubation concept. He wrote, "Incubation would consist in getting rid of false leads and hampering assumption so as to approach the problem with an 'open mind.' We can call this the forgetting-hypothesis."[1]

The effect of a pause comes from the negative pressure one experiences as a result of the halting momentum of a process. Eliot described an experience of writing as analogous to a mystical flow of poetry he felt when held captive by illness. The poetry that breaks forth, he wrote,

> gives me the impression ... of having undergone a long incubation, though we do not know until the shell breaks what kind of egg we have been sitting on. To me it seems that at these moments, which are characterized by the sudden lifting of the burden of anxiety and fear which presses upon our daily life so steadily that we are unaware of it, what happens is something negative; that is to say, not "inspiration" as we commonly think of it, but the breaking down of strong habitual barriers—which tend to re-form very quickly. Some obstruction is momentarily whisked away. The accompanying feeling is less like what we know as positive pleasure, than like a sudden relief from an intolerable burden.[2]

Your pause may be different from everyone else's pause. Each of your pauses may be different from each other. Perhaps you pause because you are held captive by something else, like traveling or being sick in bed. You may choose to do something else as a distraction from your creativity, such as doing laundry or enjoying a drink at a coffee shop, thus allowing time for ideas to blossom. Woodland went to the beach.

Carroll, the author of *Alice in Wonderland*, penned an essay in 1906 titled "Feeding the Mind" in which he compares pausing to mastication:

> First then, we should set ourselves to provide for our mind its proper kind of food....
>
> Then we should be careful to provide this wholesome food in proper amount. Mental gluttony, or over-reading, is a dangerous

propensity tending to weakness of digestive power, and in some cases to loss of appetite....

Having settled the proper kind, amount, and variety of our mental food, it remains that we should be careful to allow *proper intervals* between meal and meal, and not swallow the food hastily without mastication, so that it may be thoroughly digested; both which rules, for the body, are also applicable at once to the mind.[3]

Maybe your mind wanders, and you daydream. Jerome Singer, known as the "father of daydreaming" and a professor emeritus of psychology at the Yale School of Medicine, has written extensively on the subject. One of the "patterns" of daydreaming he identified is what he calls "positive-vivid daydreaming"—which can be the very thing to invigorate the creative process. Also referred to as "the happy daydreamer," Singer describes the pattern as "characterized by high scores on scales such as Positive Reactions to Daydreaming, Acceptance of Daydreaming, Visual Imagery in Daydreaming, Auditory Imagery in Daydreaming, Future-Oriented Daydreams, Interpersonal Curiosity, and other scales which suggest ideational interests, an active thought life and the use of daydreams for solving problems."[4] (I admit to finding it humorous that Singer does not see two other patterns of daydreaming he identifies— "Anxious Distractibility in Daydreaming" and "Guilty, Negatively Toned Emotional Daydreams"—as useful resources.)

Ostensibly, a pause is stopping work—but the creative cycle doesn't come to a halt. You may take a long pause from exhaustion or stress. You may take a momentary break simply by virtue of looking up as you turn a page. You may take an extended break as you switch a material or format, language or approach. Likewise, you may take an extended pause to abandon a movement, field, or discipline.

DeCredico, who I introduced in chapter 4, would on occasion rip up his drawings—and taught his students to do so, too. He was making an intentional break from the process by sabotaging his own work if it became predictable. The conscious break with his momentum took him away from "automatic" thinking (like preconceptions). He also gave an assignment to his students to make a self-portrait in the shower. All but one of the students responded by making representations of themselves in the shower. One student, though, actually took paper and charcoal into the shower, and drew his self-portrait with water streaming down the page. DeCredico's assignment is not unlike the pedagogical strategies I have used with my own students to derail the intentions that can sometimes overpower any discovery. The one student who accepted the challenge was on an adventure that broke with the common interpretation of the assignment. "In the shower" did not refer to what had to be depicted but rather to a confrontation with the process.

You can treat your pause as the opposite of other stages of the creative process I've discussed in earlier chapters. Instead of connecting, take a break. Not tracking, but being tracked by the exact idea, answer, insight that you were seeking and tracking. Rather than gathering, let go. Instead of paying attention, be distracted. Not propelling, but stopping the current motion of the process. "Sleep on it."

I see pausing as an opportunity to see external to the frame you have already established, to allow new stimuli to enter the creative process, to prompt another idea. It is a chance to step off the reiterative track of logical decisions. It frees you from the concrete and reintroduces abstraction. It can be the chance to transform what you are working on through connections not previously made. By stopping, for whatever length of time, you weaken your willful grip, and can become more open and more open minded.

Rosamond E. M. Harding (1898–1982) was a noted musicologist and music historian whose book on the history of the pianoforte is regarded as one of the most important works in the field. In 1942, she wrote a book titled *An Anatomy of Inspiration*. In it, she addresses the notion of pausing.

> There is much to be said in favour of laying a work aside to mature; for one thing it gives the judgment time to operate; the mind is able to return to the work from time to time with a fresh outlook; and check it from many different angles. It follows also that if new ideas are to be set aside to develop and newly finished works left to "mature," there must be several things on hand at the same time in various stages of development. The continuity of attention is purposely shortened and interrupted partly on account of the rest this gives. Sir Joseph Thomson says that new ideas "come more freely if the mind does not dwell too long on one subject without interruption" ... and partly because a change may bring about fruitful combinations of ideas. There is no doubt that it may be an advantage especially in some branches of science to turn from one thing to another, since discoveries often result from an idea from one branch of science being applied to another, as, for example, when electricity began to be used in connection with chemistry.[5]

Most important about pausing is to accept nothing, and then something.

Storm's-eye view 10.

CONTINUING

The "sands" of the Bodélé Depression of the Sahara Desert in North Africa are comprised primarily of the carcasses of plankton that once floated above in the waters of an ancient inland sea that has since dried up, specifically the silicon carcasses of diatom—a group of algae that are still today the major type of phytoplankton, or plankton that obtain food through photosynthesis. These plankton are the base of the ocean food chain and also the primary producers of the world's oxygen. Phytoplankton convert carbon dioxide into oxygen through photosynthesis. They are the lungs of our planet, and the Bodélé Depression is a giant cemetery thick with their brittle carcasses.

Midmorning, the winds tend to pick up across North Africa's deserts. The wind stirs the diatomaceous earth of the desert, and about every three days, the stirring builds into a Saharan dust storm. The brittle carcasses break easily in the wind and are carried as fine dust particles that trigger a chain reaction, producing dust storms all the way out to the Atlantic Ocean. Convective currents carry the diatom carcasses up into the clouds, sometimes falling as rain into the ocean and thus feeding the living plankton. Diatoms are nutrient rich with iron and phosphorus.

The prevailing winds carry a supply westward, eight thousand miles across the Atlantic Ocean to as far as the Peruvian rain forest. There, they dissolve in the water droplets of the daily rains, feeding the jungle's vegetation. The excess falls to the rain forest floor and is carried out in the river to the sea, as sediment, again feeding another crop of wandering plankton.

Satellite imagery shows the six-day trip of dust from the Sahara across the Atlantic to the Amazon and producing plankton blooms in the ocean. In less than a week, a cycle from death to giving life is made on a vast scale: from the depths of an ancient seabed to the cloud cover above an ocean; from east to west; from an arid desert to saturated rain forest.

The same could be said for the transformation from the release of creative processes, by pausing, abandoning, giving up, death—a cycle of life to death to life again.

Like the convective currents that pull the carcasses into a life-giving state, intuition springs from the depths of unconsciousness. Beyond our awareness, propelled by unbounded associative logic, intuition emerges with illuminating hunches. Forms emerge from the cemetery of thoughts, and feed new associations and connections that cross boundaries of procedures, disciplines, and methods.

The intuition is a little stir that springs from the unconscious. As Koestler writes,

> The intervention of unconscious processes in the creative act is a phenomenon quite different from the automatization of skills and our unawareness of the sources of inspiration is of a quite different

order from the unawareness of what we are doing while we tie our shoe strings or copy a letter on the typewriter. In the creative act there is an upward surge from some unknown fertile, underground layers of the mind, whereas the process I have described is a downward relegation of the controls of skilled techniques.[1]

BEGINNINGS

A beginning exists at the scale of the onset of one project. Or within a single project, there are new beginnings that come from approaching it with a fresh strategy, or after one work is done or as one genre of work is exhausted. A beginning happens at the onsets of cycles at many scales. There are beginnings in the middle of a single process at the scale of a single act within a process. For example, a beginning can come after you tire of using one material and try another. It can be a new beginning that one individual makes, or between one individual's work and another, or one group of individuals working on a common cause and the next.

But what precedes a beginning is the pause, a time away, a distraction, completion, destruction, or death. Something has broken the attachment, the focus, purpose, and activity. Out of the pause, distraction, death, mind wandering, or disconnect is a beginning again. Some kind of acknowledgment of a break of process, of turning away, is experienced; it is equivalent to saying good-bye and walking away. Sometimes you may leave in disgust or exhaustion or boredom, or because you are repeating yourself, going around and around, and have given up. There is a sense of negative pressure, a sense of detachment, nothing. I think that this is the most important point about beginning again: the nothingness, with no expectation, with calm. You have said "good-bye" to something or have just walked away. You have said sayonara. A beginning again is what you face after saying good-bye. Out of this calm you start (again) before you realize that you have—with something appearing quietly, unannounced.

It begins with a little stir, like the winds in the Sahara. Then something quietly takes our attention. A modest something we notice brings us away from the pause that followed turning away from whatever we were focusing on previously. This moment of recognition is almost without your knowing it because things take your attention all day. It could be a mild distraction from the pause, silence, death, or nothingness that followed the quiet departure of a previous phase of the creative process. Distractions, which seem so counterproductive to the creative process, have a role, breaking the silence and stirring the unconscious mind in a new direction. It is not something noteworthy at first, until it becomes the beginning of something. This is an event of recognition that is truly in the sense of re-cognition or re-cognating something again, as though for the first time.

It could be an entirely new line of thinking or work, or going back to the same pursuit from another perspective. These are different scales of beginnings; they are different increments of the cycle of creativity (creative practice). These cycles of beginnings are embedded in the work.

BEGINNING AGAIN, OR REBEGINNING

Henri Poincaré (1854–1912) was a French mathematician and theoretical physicist who made important contributions to several fields, including mathematical physics, celestial mechanics, and pure and applied mathematics—including the Fuchsian functions, later named automorphic functions. His description of how the ideas came to him, one after other as he engaged in other activities, has become a famous example of how ideas can spring to mind after a break from intense work. It is worth quoting at length.

> For fifteen days I strove to prove that there could not be any functions like those I have since called Fuchsian functions. I was then very ignorant; every day I seated myself at my work table, stayed an hour or two, tried a great number of combinations and reached no results. One evening, contrary to my custom, I drank black coffee and could not sleep. Ideas rose in crowds; I felt them collide until pairs interlocked, so to speak, making a stable combination. By the next morning I had established the existence of a class of Fuchsian functions, those which came from the hypergeometric series; I had only to write out the results, which took but a few hours.
>
> Then I wanted to represent these functions by the quotient of two series; this idea was perfectly conscious and deliberate; the analogy with elliptic functions guided me. I asked myself what properties these series must have if they existed, and I succeeded without difficulty in forming the series I have called theta-Fuchsian.
>
> Just at this time I left Caen, where I was then living, to go on a geologic excursion under the auspices of the school of mines. The changes of travel made me forget my mathematical work. Having reached Coutances, we entered an omnibus to go some place or other. At the moment when I put my foot on the step the idea came to me, without anything in my former thoughts seeming to have paved the way for it, that the transformations I had used to define the Fuchsian functions were identical with those of non-Euclidean

geometry. I did not verify the idea; I should not have had time, as upon taking my seat in the omnibus, I went on with a conversation already commenced, but I felt a perfect certainty. On my return to Caen, for conscience' sake, I verified the result at my leisure.

Then I turned my attention to the study of some arithmetical questions apparently without much success and without a suspicion of any connection with my preceding researches. Disgusted with my failure, I went to spend a few days at the seaside, and thought of something else. One morning, walking on the bluff, the idea came to me, with just the same characteristics of brevity, suddenness and immediate certainty, that the arithmetic transformations of indeterminate ternary quadratic forms were identical with those of non-Euclidean geometry.

Returned to Caen, I meditated on this result and deduced the consequences. The example of quadratic forms showed me that they were Fuchsian functions other than those corresponding to the hypergeometric series; I saw that I could apply to them the theory of theta-Fuchsian functions other than those from the hypergeometric series, the ones I then knew. Naturally I set myself to form all these functions. I made a systematic attack upon them and carried all the outworks, one after another. There was one however that still held out, whose fall would involve that of the whole place. But all my efforts only served at first the better to show me the difficulty, which was indeed something. All this work was perfectly conscious.

Thereupon I left for Mont-Valerian, where I was to go through my military service; so I was very differently occupied. One day, going along the street, the solution of the difficulty which had stopped me suddenly appeared to me. I did not try to go deep into it immediately, and only after my service did I again take up the question. I had all the elements and had only to arrange them and put them together.

So I wrote out my final memoir at a single stroke and without difficulty.[2]

In essence, Poincaré was describing rebeginnings that come out of distractions. When you are too set on finding something, you may miss something else. Distracted states are states in which a new open mind is possible.

Poincaré's experience mirrors Feynman's story about the plate in chapter 3. Feynman solved a problem—a solution that earned him a Nobel Prize—as he was distracted in the related setting of a cafeteria.

REBEGINNING OUT OF FORGETTING AND FROM "FAILURE"

Perhaps you have read *The Name of the Rose* (*Il nome della rosa*), the best-selling novel by the Italian semiotician Umberto Eco (b. 1932). In it, there is a mysterious manuscript that contains the lost second book of Aristotle's *Poetics*, with pages that have been poisoned so they will kill anyone who touches them. Eco credits a book he bought as a youth—forgotten about, only to be found in his house later—as the inspiration for the physical description he gives of the mysterious manuscript: "But by a sort of internal camera I photographed those pages, and for decades the image of those poisonous leaves lied in the most remote part of my soul, as in a grave, until the moment it emerged again (I do not know for which reasons) and I believed to have invented it."[3]

Eco goes on to describe in more detail how the book came to be that inspiration. After the publication of *The Name of the Rose*,

I started to be more frequently in touch with librarians and book collectors (and certainly because I had a little more money at my disposal) I became a regular rare books collector. It had happened before, in the course of my life, that I bought some old book, but by chance, and only when they were very cheap.... Only in the last decade I have become a serious book collector, and "serious" means that one has to consult specialized catalogues and must write, for every book, a technical file, with the collation, historical information on the previous or following editions, and a precise description of the physical state of the copy. This last job requires a technical jargon, in order to precisely name foxed, browned, waterstained, soiled, washed or crisp leaves, cropped margins, erasures, re-baked bindings, rubbed joints and so on.

One day, rummaging through the upper shelves of my home library I discovered an edition of the *Poetics of Aristotle*, commented by Antonio Riccoboni, Padova 1587. I had forgot to have it.... I bought it ... probably twenty or more years before....

Then I started writing my description. I copied the title page and I discovered that the edition had an Appendix, "Ejusdem Ars Comica ex Aristotele." This means that Riccoboni tried to re-construct the lost second book of the *Poetics*. It was not however an unusual endeavor, and I went on to set up the physical description of the copy. Then it happened to me what happened to a certain Zatesky described by Lurja, who, having lost part of his brain during the war, and with part of the brain the whole of his memory and of his speaking ability, was nevertheless still able to write: thus automatically his hand wrote down all the information he was unable to think of, and step by step he reconstructed his own identity by reading what he was writing.

Likewise, I was looking coldly and technically at the book, writing my description, and suddenly I realized that I was re-writing

The Name of the Rose. The only difference was that from page 120, when the *Ars Comica* begins, the lower and not the upper margins were severely damaged; but all the rest was the same, the pages progressively browned and dampstained at the end stuck together, and looked as if they were ointed with a disgusting fat substance. I had in my hands, in printed form, the manuscript I described in my novel. I had had it for years and years at my reach, at home.

At a first moment I thought of an extraordinary coincidence; then I was tempted to believe in a miracle; at the end I decided that *Wo Es war, soll Ich warden* [a famous declaration by Sigmund Freud, meaning "Where it was, shall I be"]. I bought that book in my youth, I skimmed through it, I realized that it was exaggeratedly soiled, I put it somewhere and I forgot it. But by a sort of internal camera I photographed those pages, and for decades the image of those poisonous leaves lied in the most remote part of my soul, as in a grave, until the moment it emerged again (I do not know for which reasons) and I believed to have invented it.

Despite the break in awareness, processes continue and transform our thinking. It is as though thoughts are incorporated and embodied. In chapter 4, I wrote, "A creative work is a condensation of its making. What you put into it stays there and speaks for you." Can the same be said for us and our making? Are memories embodied? Can conceptualization be embodied and transformed? Can these immaterial things become a part of our physical selves so that the emergence of them again (after the death, after the burial of pausing) is a natural process? Through embodiment, is the dry air of concepts humidified? Do the humid embodied thoughts, memories, and dreams burst into the colder air of awareness and condense into a cloud?

Eco's rebeginning came from forgetting, but Jobs's rebeginning came from losing his job. In May 1985, John Sculley—then Apple's CEO—removed Jobs from his managerial duties as head of the company's Macintosh division. Sculley had been given that authority by the Apple board of directors the previous month. It was quite a blow to Jobs, who was an Apple founder.

In his 2005 commencement address at Stanford University, Jobs said being fired from Apple was "the best thing that could have ever happened to me. The heaviness of being successful was replaced by the lightness of being a beginner again, less sure about everything. It freed me to enter one of the most creative periods of my life." He added, "I'm pretty sure none of this would have happened if I hadn't been fired from Apple. It was awful-tasting medicine, but I guess the patient needed it."[4]

THE BEGINNER'S MIND AND NONATTACHMENT

In *Zen Mind, Beginner's Mind*, a collection of talks by Zen master Shunryu Suzuki (1904–1971), the author spoke of keeping a "beginner's mind" at all stages of life. In fact, he defined having a beginner's mind as a way of life. To Suzuki, this meant retaining the innocent, open, natural, inquiring mind of a beginner, a mind free from doubt, cynicism, and mindless habit. "It is a wisdom which is seeking for wisdom," he said. "It is empty of expectations and demands and accepts what is."[5]

This concept of a beginner's mind fits well with the emergence of a beginning from a pause in the creative process. The relevance is clear if we think of beginnings that emerge from the pause as a process that can be sustained. Instead of a beginning being understood as a point in time or fleeting moment, it can be practiced with vary-ing durations. The state of a beginning can be seen in creative prac-tices as well as in Zen practice.

Key to this is the notion of something new coming out of nonat-tachment. As Suzuki said in defining "true nonattachment," "We should forget, day by day, what we have done … and we should do something new."

His advice is probably the most succinct for maintaining the beginner's mind and being creative. It refers back to the idea of unlearning or forgetting presented in chapter 2. It is the only way you can gain wisdom through a creative practice without the channels of practice hardening into a set track that limits specu-lation. Discovery and invention happen outside the existing tracks or matrices of thought within a discipline. Nonattachment comes with a break in the process—or a pause—throughout the creative cycling. As Suzuki put it, "When you give up, when you no longer want something, or when you do not try to do anything special, then you do something."

The power of the pause is nonattachment to precisely what you were attached to before taking a pause. That is what you've "given up." A gift is something you no longer feel attached to that can be passed on to another. To give, as Suzuki said, is nonattachment.

The nonattachment of "giving up" seems to be linked to the arrival of gifts. They may come in the form of a notion from within or as something external that takes one's quiet attention, one's curi-osity without a sense of what is at stake, because there is no sense of attachment.

Creative practices have a greater and lesser dedication to the state of naturalness of the beginner's mind. Suzuki explained *naturalness* as "some feeling of being independent from everything, or some activity which is based on nothingness. Something which comes out of nothing is naturalness, like a seed or plant coming out of the ground.... And as it grows in the course of time, it expresses its nature."

Performance artists strive for a sustained naturalness, a pure expression, whether their performance is improvisational or scripted. Even when working from a script and weeks of drills, memorizing lines and blocking out movements on a stage, actors find their way in the moment with each performance of what is at stake with their character with each line in each scene, with the other actors, the setting, and the audience. Although memorized and delivered again and again, each line of the script is *discovered* from the emotions that arise in the moment, making a monologue, scene, and play a journey that is a unique and natural outcome of that iteration.

For an athlete, although a move may be drilled over and over in practice to maximize its precise delivery, when it comes to the actual athletic performance, that move needs to be as natural as the instinct with which an animal would move, without question or hesitation. This is the upward and downward traffic about which Koestler wrote. All the preparation, the actor's memorization of the script, the muscle memory of the athlete, allows certain things to become habitual, to be *forgotten* by the conscious mind, so one can be freed to be aware of the moment. Artists of all kinds, designers, scientists, and engineers—they all have stages within their practice that are, for lack of a better word, felt with the fullest awareness of the moment. The duration of these stages may be far less than the duration of a play or performance or race, but it is still a part of the process that is prepared for and then forgotten.

GIVING UP COMPLETELY

There is risk in giving up completely. The longer the pause, the more difficult it is to continue. The nonattachment is a loss of momentum, interest, and passion. Your personal psychology plays a role in how you are likely to respond to pauses that come from failures. The recognition of new input is often the only reason why you return to a work after a longer pause. But it is not easy to recognize the new beginnings, because they typically come as beginnings in their infancy. They also are unfamiliar. We are all stricken with the tendency to reject previously unrecognized connections. The matrices of thought can be woven tightly over time in our conscious minds, and discoveries that don't fit the existing matrices seem mistaken and illogical.

Koestler wrote about this in another of his books: "Some of the greatest discoveries ... consist mainly in the clearing away of psychological roadblocks which obstruct the approach to reality; which is why, *post factum*, they appear so obvious."[6] I have seen thousands of projects start and stop, succeed and fail. I am familiar with these patterns of the stages. Despite the real discouragement I feel from failures, knowing and believing in the unfamiliar that comes from the uncertainty of being shipwrecked is what keeps me going, and what I hope to share with my students and you.

Of course, I realize it is wishful thinking to expect that anyone, or any more than a handful of readers, approached this book by opening it randomly and beginning to read from here rather than from chapter 1. Nevertheless, I ask you to pause and reflect on the elements in these chapters as a mix, not as steps, so you can engage with creative practice in a way you probably have before but never thought about until now. If you can clear your mind, I am confident you will recognize this stormlike process in your own creative practice. Awareness of uncertainty as your friend will help you navigate genuine creativity. You will make problems that get you going and a language that gets you running. You will find that you can see ahead and find new "solutions." And you will make the transformation into the next cycle.

PART OF A CONTINUUM

As I have written throughout these chapters, creativity is a reiterative process. But it does not reiterate within a closed loop until some end is achieved. It is ongoing, continuing. As in a storm, there may be millions of rotations or zillions of "cycles" of water vapor carried up, condensing, forming a band of rain, and raining down. I see the stages of creativity as I've described them in this book as happening once, several, or many times in the life span of a given creative work, but that the work itself is not an end point of creativity, only of a particular "project." At any point in creative practice, you may go "back" and unlearn, or go "back" and gather.

And just like a storm is never really over, because as the wind and rain abate, the storm is sowing the seeds of its own renewal, the creative process, too, continues. The storm eventually "dies," but the hydrologic cycle continues. Ocean water fuels a storm, which is emptied out as rain over land. The saturated land evaporates its moisture or loses it through runoff back to the sea. And just as a storm scatters, diffracts, and retracts but never ends, so too does creativity continue. In my observation, in fact, the continuation of the creative process is immutable.

The "output" of creativity, the reaching of the goal or ideal, and thus the making of some product or consequence, is not an end point. This holds true whether the creativity takes place in an artistic or scientific realm, whether in engineering or design, whether a medical diagnosis or the writing of a poem. Creativity continues; an artifact formed through creative practice is not an end point but rather a point along a never-ending way. Because it is continual, creativity is a virtuous circle. That term refers to a condition in which a favorable circumstance or result gives rise to another that subsequently supports the first. It is a cycle of interdependent events.

The helix can be described as comprising the stages of the creative process. Again, the order is somewhat arbitrary. You unlearn to rid yourself of preconceptions, which creates the need/want to know. Your need makes a problem, which you define and redefine, and then you move forward to gather and track that with which you will solve the problem. You propel forward with the language of your creative endeavor into perception, from which you derive conception. With your concept, you move forward still, seeing ahead with your imagination. Through all this, you reiterate back into different phases of the creative process, in and out until you can transform quantity into quality by connecting all the material you have gathered and giving it meaning. Your goal looms ahead, but again it will not be an end point.

In chapter 2, I quoted Eliot from his "Four Quartets." He is relevant again:

What we call the beginning is often the end
And to make an end is to make a beginning.
The end is where we start from....
We shall not cease from exploration
And the end of all our exploring
Will be to arrive where we started
And know the place for the first time.
Through the unknown, unremembered gate
When the last of earth left to discover
Is that which was the beginning[7]

In the introduction I wrote that my students often ask, "How do you know? How do you know what to do, where to go, when it's right?" and I said that this book is my response to that question. The permission to enter the "unknown, unremembered gate" comes from realizing that you don't know. Wanting to know something that you do not know is the creative process.

NOTES

INTRODUCTION

1. Robinson, *Out of Our Minds.*

2. Ponge, *The Making of the Pré.*

CHAPTER 1

1. Whitman, "Song of Occupations."

CHAPTER 2

1. Epictetus, *Discourses* II:17.

2. Gell-Mann, *Quark and the Jaguar*, chap. 17.

3. Keats, "Letter to George and Thomas Keats."

4. Ortega y Gasset, *Dehumanization of Art and Other Essays.*

5. Klee, "Creative Credo."

6. Fox, "N. Joseph Woodland, Inventor of the Bar Code, Dies at 91."

7. Fitzgerald, *Great Gatsby*.

8. Selinger, "Creative Engineer."

9. Eliot, "Four Quartets."

10. Academy of Achievement, "Murray Gell-Mann Interview."

11. Bachelard, *Poetics of Space*.

12. Dhawan, "Business Schools Need to Focus on Unlearning."

CHAPTER 3

1. Hugo, *Triggering Town*.

2. Bachelard, *Poetics of Space*.

3. Gell-Mann, *Quark and the Jaguar*.

4. Feynman, *Surely You're Joking, Mr. Feynman!*

CHAPTER 4

1. Wilson, *The Hand*.

2. Personal correspondence with the author.

3. LaBarre, "How Infographics Guru Nicholas Felton Inspired Facebook's Timeline."

4. Azvolinsky, "Birds of a Feather."

5. *Newsweek* Staff, "All Eyes on Google."

6. DeCredico, "Artist Statements."

7. Hugo, *Triggering Town*.

8. Chopra, *Seven Spiritual Laws of Success*.

CHAPTER 5

1. Wilson, "Does Sign Language Solve the Chomsky Problem?"

2. Klee, "Creative Credo."

3. Olson, "Projective Verse."

CHAPTER 6

1. Koestler, *Act of Creation*.

2. Rozendaal and Knoek van Soest, "Optical Acceleration Cancellation."

3. Grab, "Gravity Glue."

4. Personal correspondence with the author, February 2013.

5. Peers, "Field Study."

6. Chabris and Simons, *Invisible Gorilla* (emphasis added).

7. James, "Hidden Self."

8. Koestler, *Act of Creation*, 191.

9. Hadamard, *Mathematician's Mind*.

10. Koestler, *Act of Creation*.

CHAPTER 7

1. Carroll, "Wool and Water."

2. Bachelard, *The Poetics of Space*.

3. Personal correspondence with the author, February 21, 2015.

4. Blazer, *Aqua Firma*.

5. Pound, *Gaudier-Brzeska*.

6. After the first edition of this book was published, the painter and RISD professor Nicholas Evans-Cato (mentioned on pages 89 to 90) did extensive research on recreating John Schroeder's object. His recreated objects as instruments for reflecting color, as did John's: Shadowed areas fall in the blue end of the spectrum while reflected light falls in the warmer end. He was not able to get the intensity of John's image, which is due in a large part to the property of Kodachrome slide film, known to intensify the saturation of color, especially colors that fall within the warm end of the spectrum.

7. Eliot, "Four Quartets."

CHAPTER 8

1. Wolf, "Steve Jobs."

2. Darwin, *On the Origin of Species*.

3. Gould, *Dinosaur in a Haystack*.

4. Smith, *Wealth of Nations*.

5. Quoted in Gould, *Ever Since Darwin*.

6. Quoted in Henn, "At 30, the Original Mac Is Still an Archetype of Innovation."

7. Zimmer, "In the Human Brain, Size Really Isn't Everything."

8. Koestler, *Act of Creation*.

9. Ibid.

10. Ibid.

11. Hillman, *The Soul's Code.*

12. Personal communication with the author.

13. Carroll, "Wool and Water."

14. Jung, "Synchronicity."

15. Schopenhauer, *World as Will and Representation.*

CHAPTER 9

1. Hadamard, *Mathematician's Mind.*

2. Eliot, *Use of Poetry and the Use of Criticism.*

3. Carroll, "Feeding the Mind."

4. Singer, *Inner World of Daydreaming.*

5. Harding, *Anatomy of Inspiration.*

CHAPTER 10

1. Koestler, *Act of Creation.*

2. Poincaré, "Description of His Own Creativity."

3. Eco, "Author and His Interpreters."

4. Jobs, Stanford University Commencement Address.

5. Suzuki, *Zen Mind, Beginner's Mind.*

6. Koestler, *Sleepwalkers.*

7. Eliot, "Four Quartets."

Academy of Achievement. "Murray Gell-Mann Interview." December 16, 1990. http://www.achievement.org/autodoc/page/geloint-1 (accessed February 20, 2015).

Azvolinsky, Anna. "Birds of a Feather ... Track Seven Neighbors to Flock Together." *News at Princeton*, February 7, 2013. http://www.princeton. edu/main/news/archive/S36/02/56I00/index.xml?section=topstories (accessed February 20, 2015).

Bachelard, Gaston. *The Poetics of Space*. New York: Orion Press, 1964. First published 1958, in French as *La Poétique de l'Espace*.

Blazer, Stuart. *Aqua Firma*. Providence, RI: Associação Cultural Burra de Milho, Terceira Island, and Gávea-Brown Publications, Brown University, 2011.

Carroll, Lewis. "Feeding the Mind." Unpublished essay, May 1906. http://www.harpers.org/sponsor/balvenie/lewis-carroll.1.html (accessed February 22, 2015).

Carroll, Lewis. "Wool and Water." In *Through the Looking Glass (and What Alice Found There)*. London: Macmillan and Co., 1871. http://www. literature.org/authors/carroll-lewis/through-the-looking-glass/chapter-05. html (accessed February 21, 2015).

Chabris, Christopher, and Daniel Simons. *The Invisible Gorilla: How Our Intuitions Deceive Us*. New York: Harmony, 2010.

Chopra, Deepak. *The Seven Spiritual Laws of Success: A Practical Guide to the Fulfillment of Your Dreams*. New York: New World Library, 1994.

Darwin, Charles. *On the Origin of Species by Means of Natural Selection, or the Preservation of Favoured Races in the Struggle for Life*. London: John Murray, 1859.

DeCredico, Alfred. "Artist Statements." http://www.decredico.com/artist-statements (accessed February 20, 2015).

Dhawan, Erica. "Business Schools Need to Focus on Unlearning." *Forbes*, June 13, 2012. http://www.forbes.com/sites/85broads/2012/06/13/deck-business-schools-must-teach-unlearning (accessed February 20, 2015).

Eco, Umberto. "The Author and His Interpreters." Lecture at the Italian Academy for Advanced Studies in America, 1996. http://www.themodernword.com/eco/eco_author.html (accessed February 20, 2015).

Eliot, T. S. "Four Quartets." In *The Complete Poems and Plays: 1909–1950*. Boston: Houghton Mifflin Harcourt, 1971.

Eliot, T. S. *The Use of Poetry and the Use of Criticism: Studies in the Relation of Criticism to Poetry in England*. Cambridge, MA: Harvard University Press, 1986. (The book is a collection of the 1932–1933 Norton Lectures at Harvard University.)

Epictetus. *The Discourses of Epictetus, Book II*. Chap. 17. Trans. George Long. London: George Bell and Sons, 1800.

Feynman, Richard P. *Surely You're Joking, Mr. Feynman!* New York: W. W. Norton and Company, 1985.

Fitzgerald, F. Scott. *The Great Gatsby*. New York: Charles Scribner's Sons, 1925.

Fox, Margalit. "N. Joseph Woodland, Inventor of the Bar Code, Dies at 91," *New York Times*, December 12, 2012. http://www.nytimes.com/2012/12/13/business/n-joseph-woodland-inventor-of-the-bar-code-dies-at-91.html?_r=0 (accessed May 7, 2015).

Gell-Mann, Murray. *The Quark and the Jaguar*. New York: W. H. Freeman and Company, 1994.

Gould, Stephen Jay. *Dinosaur in a Haystack: Reflections in Natural History*. New York: Harmony, 1995.

Gould, Stephen Jay. *Ever Since Darwin: Reflections in Natural History*. New York: W. W. Norton and Company, 1977.

Grab, Michael. "Gravity Glue." http://www.gravityglue.com/about (accessed February 21, 2015).

Hadamard, Jacques. *The Mathematician's Mind: The Psychology of Invention in the Mathematical Field*. Princeton, NJ: Princeton University Press, 1996. First published 1945.

Harding, Rosamond E. M. *An Anatomy of Inspiration*. London: W. Heffer and Sons Ltd., 1942.

Henn, Steve. "At 30, the Original Mac Is Still an Archetype of Innovation." NPR, January 24, 2013. http://www.npr.org/blogs/alltechconsidered/2014/01/24/265238567/at-30-the-original-mac-is-still-an-archetype-of-innovation (accessed February 21, 2015).

Hillman, James. *The Soul's Code: In Search of Character and Calling*. New York: Random House, 1996.

Hugo, Richard. *The Triggering Town: Lectures and Essays on Poetry and Writing*. New York: W. W. Norton and Company, 2010. First published 1979.

James, William. "The Hidden Self." In *The Heart of William James*, ed. Robert D. Richardson. Cambridge, MA: Harvard University Press, 2012. Essay first published 1890.

Jobs, Steve. Stanford University Commencement Address. http://news.stanford.edu/news/2005/june15/jobs-061505.html (accessed February 21, 2015).

Jung, Carl Gustav. "Synchronicity: An Acausal Connecting Principle." In *Collected Works of C. G. Jung*. Vol. 8. Princeton, NJ: Princeton University Press, 2010. First published 1952.

Keats, John. "Letter to George and Thomas Keats." December 28, 1817. http://en.wikisource.org/wiki/Letter_to_George_and_Thomas_Keats,_December_28,_1817 (accessed February 20, 2015).

Klee, Paul. "Creative Credo." In *Paul Klee Notebooks*, trans. Ralph Manheim. New York: Overlook Press, 1992.

Koestler, Arthur. *The Act of Creation: A Study of Conscious and Unconscious Processes of Humor, Scientific Discovery, and Art*. New York: Macmillan Company, 1964.

Koestler, Arthur. *The Sleepwalkers: A History of Man's Changing Vision of the Universe*. New York: Macmillan, 1959.

LaBarre, Suzanne. "How Infographics Guru Nicholas Felton Inspired Facebook's Timeline." *Fast Company CoDesign*, September 22, 2011. http://www.fastcodesign.com/1665062/how-infographics-guru-nicholas-felton-inspired-facebooks-timeline (accessed February 20, 2015).

Newsweek Staff. "All Eyes on Google." *Newsweek*, March 28, 2004. http://www.thedailybeast.com/newsweek/2004/03/29/all-eyes-on-google.html (accessed February 20, 2015).

Olson, Charles. "Projective Verse." In *Collected Prose*, ed. Donald Allen and Benjamin Friedlander. Berkeley: University of California Press, 1997. Essay first published 1950, as a pamphlet.

Ortega y Gasset, José. *The Dehumanization of Art and Other Essays on Art, Culture, and Literature*, trans. Willard R. Trask. Princeton, NJ: Princeton University Press, 1968. First published 1935, in Spanish.

Peers, Gordon. "Field Study." RISD European Honors Program, 1962.

Poincaré, Henri. "A Description of His Own Creativity." Trans. G. B. Halstead. 1908. http://www.is.wayne.edu/DRBOWEN/CRTVYW99/POINCARE.HTM (accessed February 16, 2015).

Ponge, Francis. *The Making of the Pré*. Trans. Lee Fahnestock. Columbia, MO: University of Missouri Press, 1979.

Pound, Ezra. *Gaudier-Brzeska: A Memoir*. New York: New Directions, 1970. First published 1916, in London by John Lane.

Robinson, Ken. *Out of Our Minds: Learning to Be Creative*. 2nd ed.Mankato, MN: Capstone, 2011.

Rozendaal, Leonard A., and A. J. Knoek van Soest. "Optical Acceleration Cancellation: A Viable Interception Strategy?" *Biological Cybernetics* 89, no. 6 (2003): 415–425.

Schopenhauer, Arthur. *The World as Will and Representation*. 2nd ed. Leipzig: F. A. Brockhaus, 1844.

Selinger, Carl. "The Creative Engineer: What Can You Do to Spark New Ideas?" *IEEE Spectrum* 41, no. 8 (2004): 47–49.

Singer, Jerome L. *The Inner World of Daydreaming*. New York: Harper and Row, 1975.

Smith, Adam. *An Inquiry into the Nature and Causes of the Wealth of Nations*. London: Strahan and Cadell, 1776.

Suzuki, Shunryu. *Zen Mind, Beginner's Mind*. Boston: Shambhala Library, 2006. First published 1970.

Whitman, Walt. "A Song of Occupations." In *Leaves of Grass*. Facsimile ed. New York: Eakins Press, 1966. First published 1855.

Wilson, Frank R. "Does Sign Language Solve the Chomsky Problem?" In *The Study of Signed Language: Essays in Honor of William C. Stokoe*, ed. David

F. Armstrong, Michael A. Karchmer, and John Vickrey Van Cleve. Washington, DC: Gallaudet University Press, 2002.

Wilson, Frank R. *The Hand: How Its Use Shapes the Brain, Language, and Human Culture.* New York: Pantheon, 1998.

Wolf, Gary. "Steve Jobs: The Next Insanely Great Thing." *Wired*, February 1996. http://www.wired.com/wired/archive/4.02/jobs_pr.html (accessed February 20, 2015).

Zimmer, Carl. "In the Human Brain, Size Really Isn't Everything." *New York Times*, December 26, 2013. http://www.nytimes.com/2013/12/26/science/in-the-human-brain-size-really-isnt-everything.html?_r=0 (accessed February 21, 2015).

All chapter opening illustrations by Kyna Leski

6 Source unknown

21 Wire structure by James Viscardi. Photo by Mark Johnston

22 Wire structure by James Viscardi. Photos by Mark Johnston

23 Wire structure by Jenny Su-Hyun Kwon. Photos by Mark Johnston

24 Wire structure by Ethan Barlow. Photo by Mark Johnston

32 Sagrada Família, from http://commons.wikimedia.org/wiki/
File:Sagrada_Familia_01.jpg. Photo by Bernard Gagnon

52 "Gravity Suit" by Jacob Wangh Knowles

53 Photo by Kyna Leski

55 Photo by Andrea Cavagna, Institute for Complex Systems (CNR), Rome

60 Plan of Baker House by Alvar Aalto, Alvar Aalto Museum

61 Alvar Aalto bent laminated wood studies, Alvar Aalto Museum

67 Turned wooden bowl designed by Kyna Leski for Drefox, Gustav Melzer, Vienna, Austria

77 Photo by Kyna Leski

79 Interior de la maqueta polifunicular para la iglesia de la Colonia Güell, Museo de la Sagrada Família

90 Untitled 6" × 8" oil painting by Nicholas Evans-Cato. Photo by Nicholas Evans-Cato

90 Oil painting by Nicholas Evans-Cato. Photo by Nicholas Evans-Cato

99 *The Battle of San Romano* by Paolo Uccello, National Gallery, London

100 *Diamond Pointed Sphere* by Paolo Uccello. Pen, ink, and brown wash, 27 × 24.5 cm. Paris, Louvre, Departement des Arts, circa 1460s

106 Watercolor painting by Kyna Leski

109 Illustration by Kyna Leski

112 Diagrams courtesy of 3six0 Architecture, Providence, Rhode Island

113 Renderings courtesy of Shepherd of the Valley Methodist Church, Hope, Rhode Island

115 Photo by John Horner, John Horner Photography, Boston, Massachusetts

115 Model by John Schroeder. Photo by Kyna Leski

138 Illustration by Kyna Leski

148 Photo by Erin Hasley

INDEX